50 Geometric Pattern Coloring Book for Adult

This Book Belongs To :

....

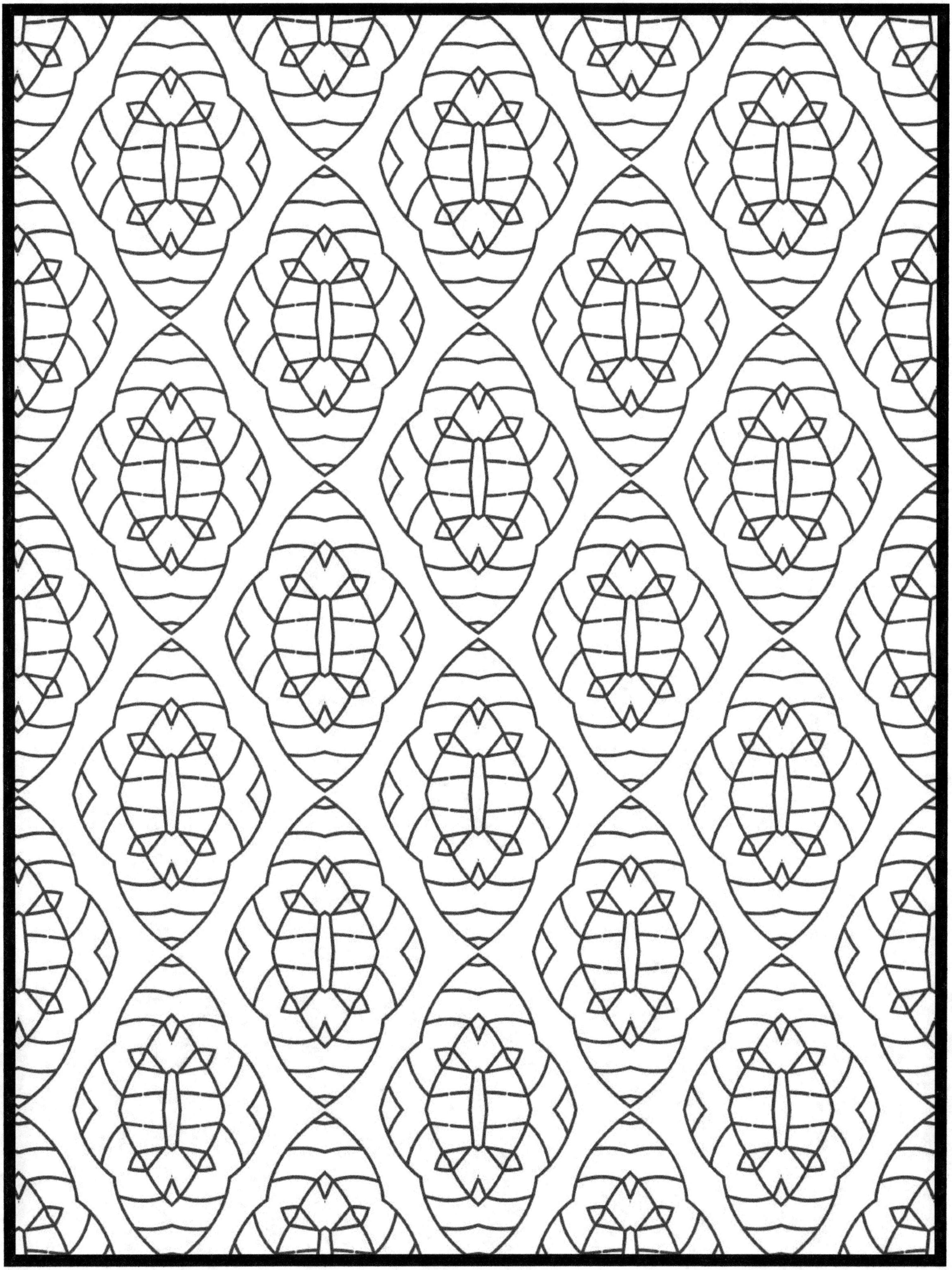

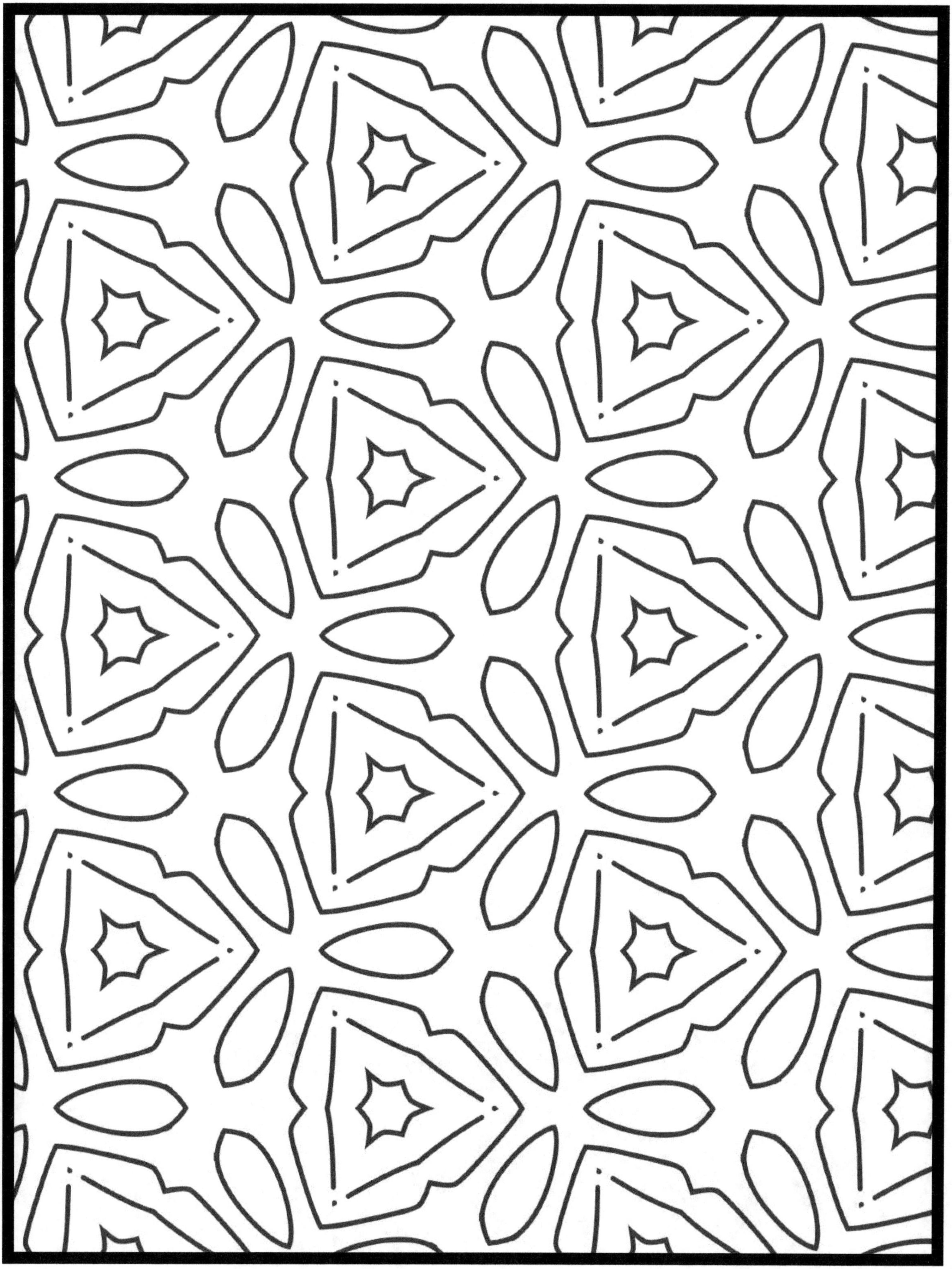

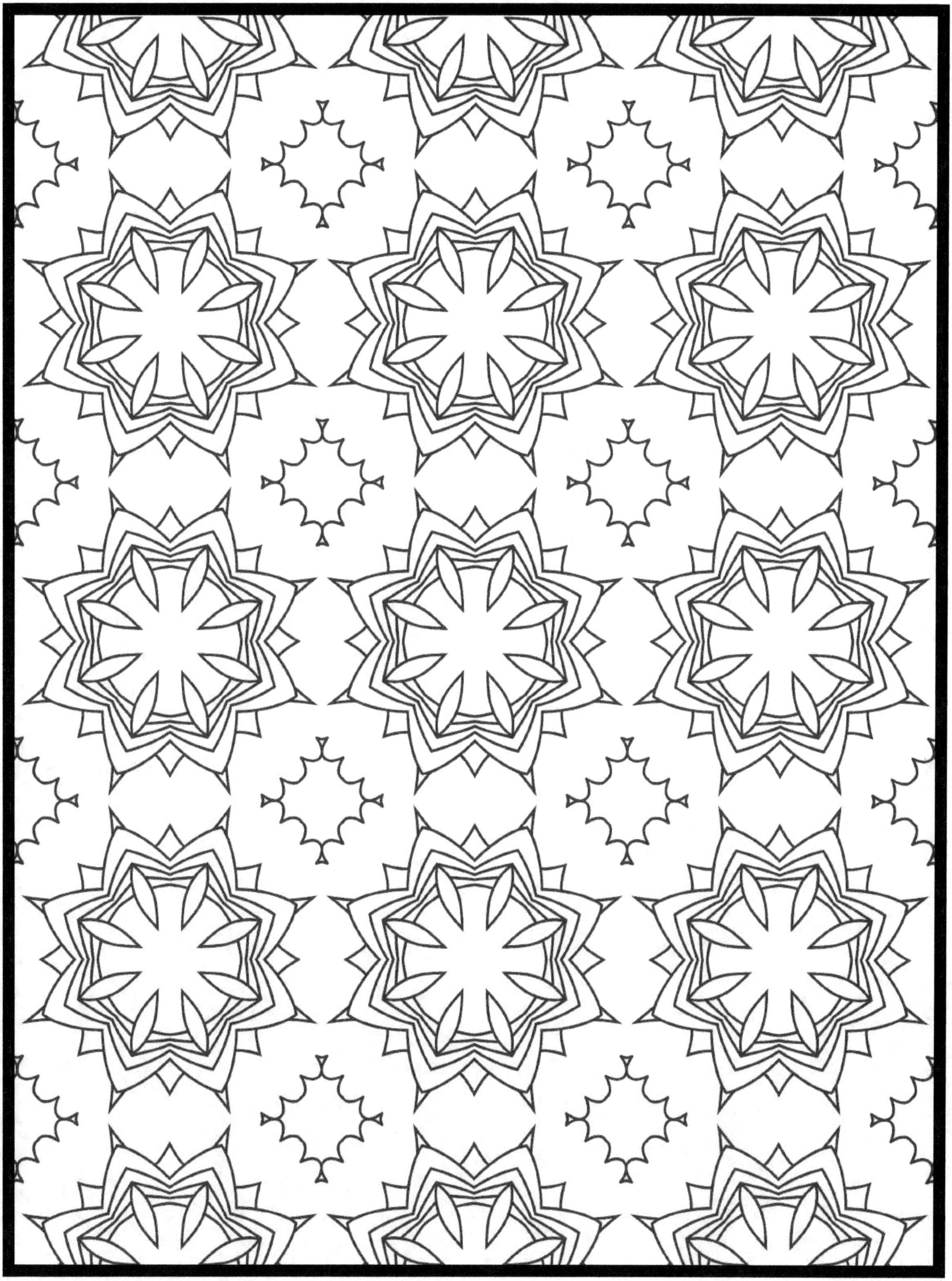

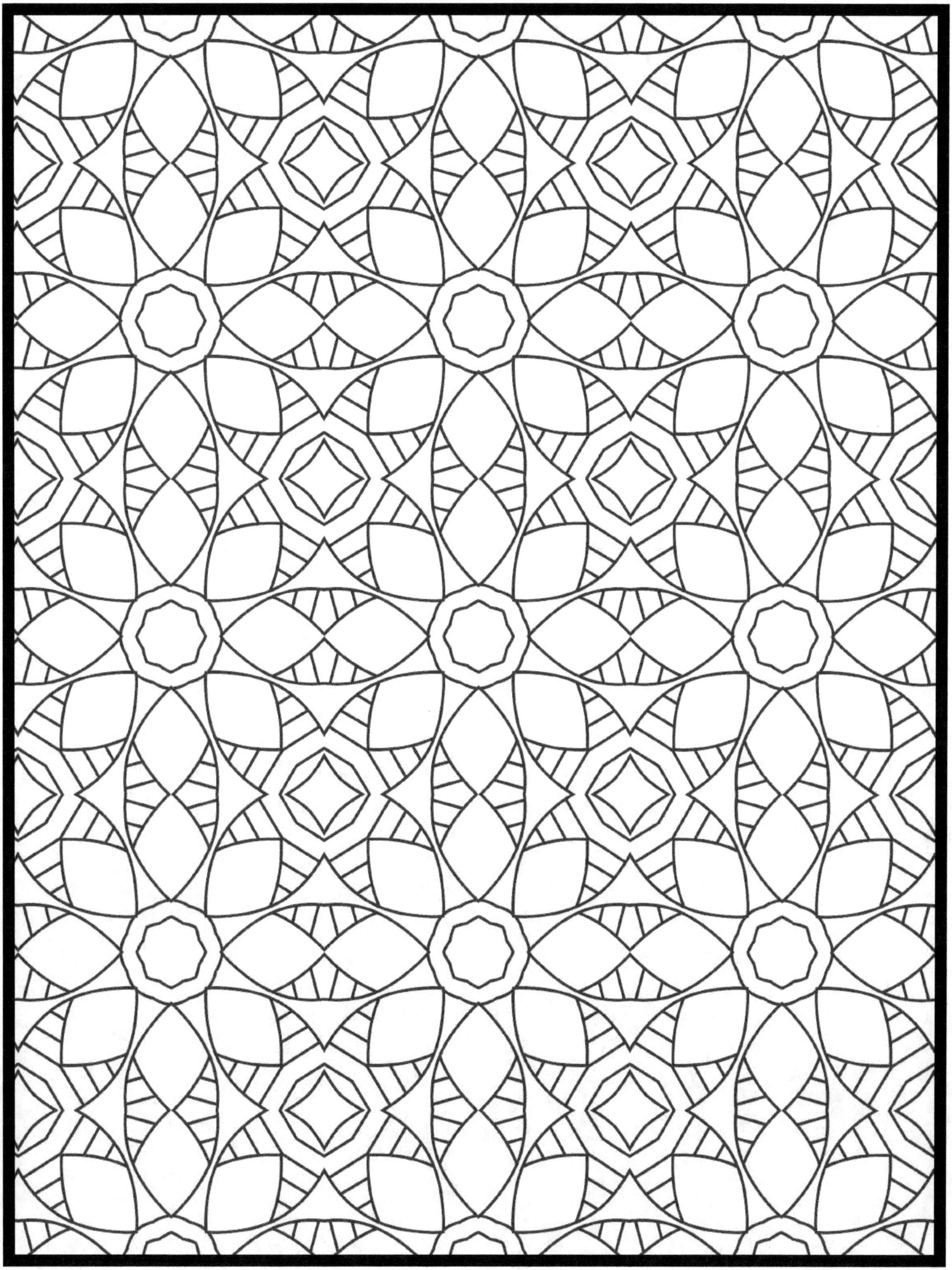

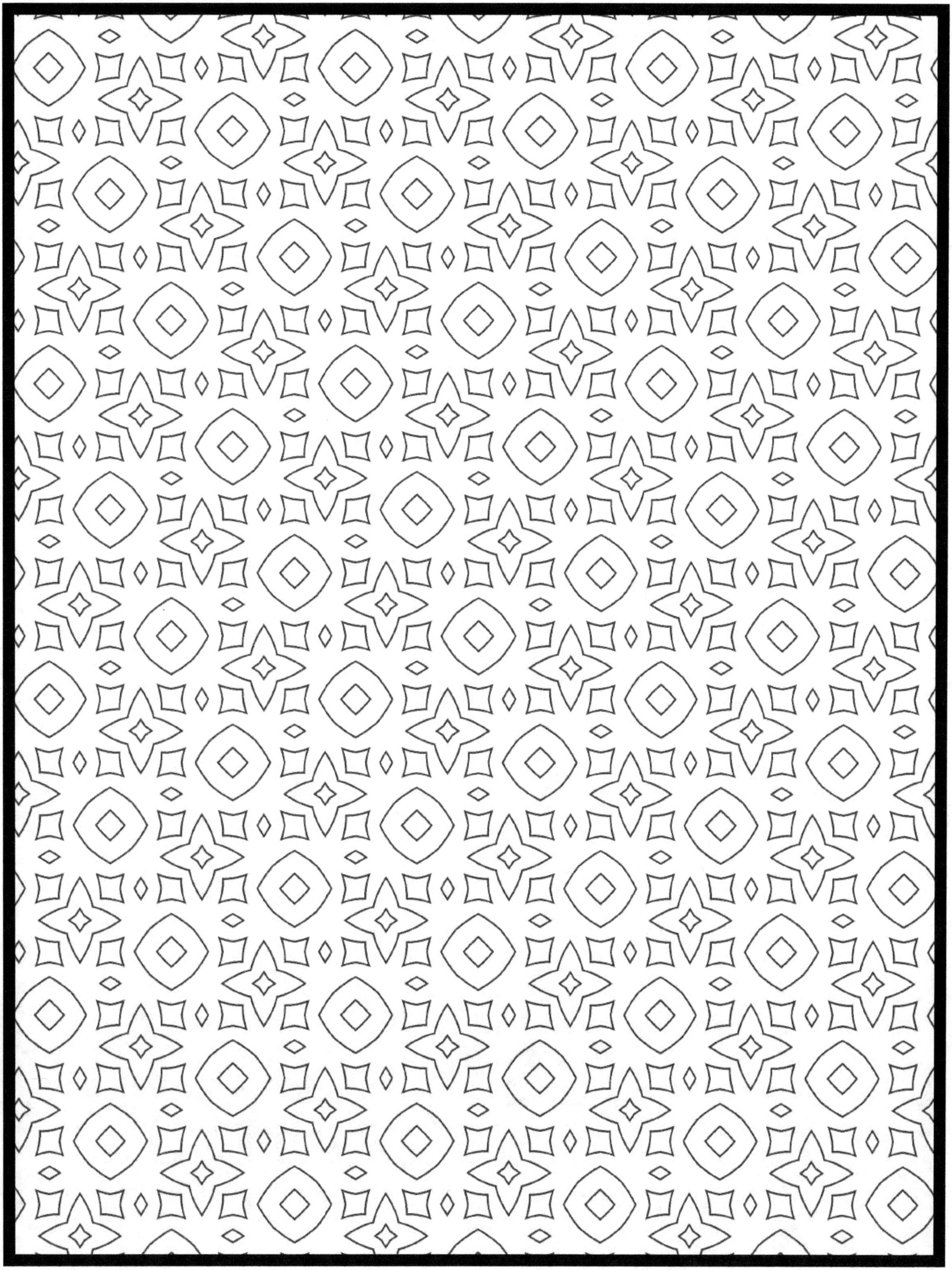

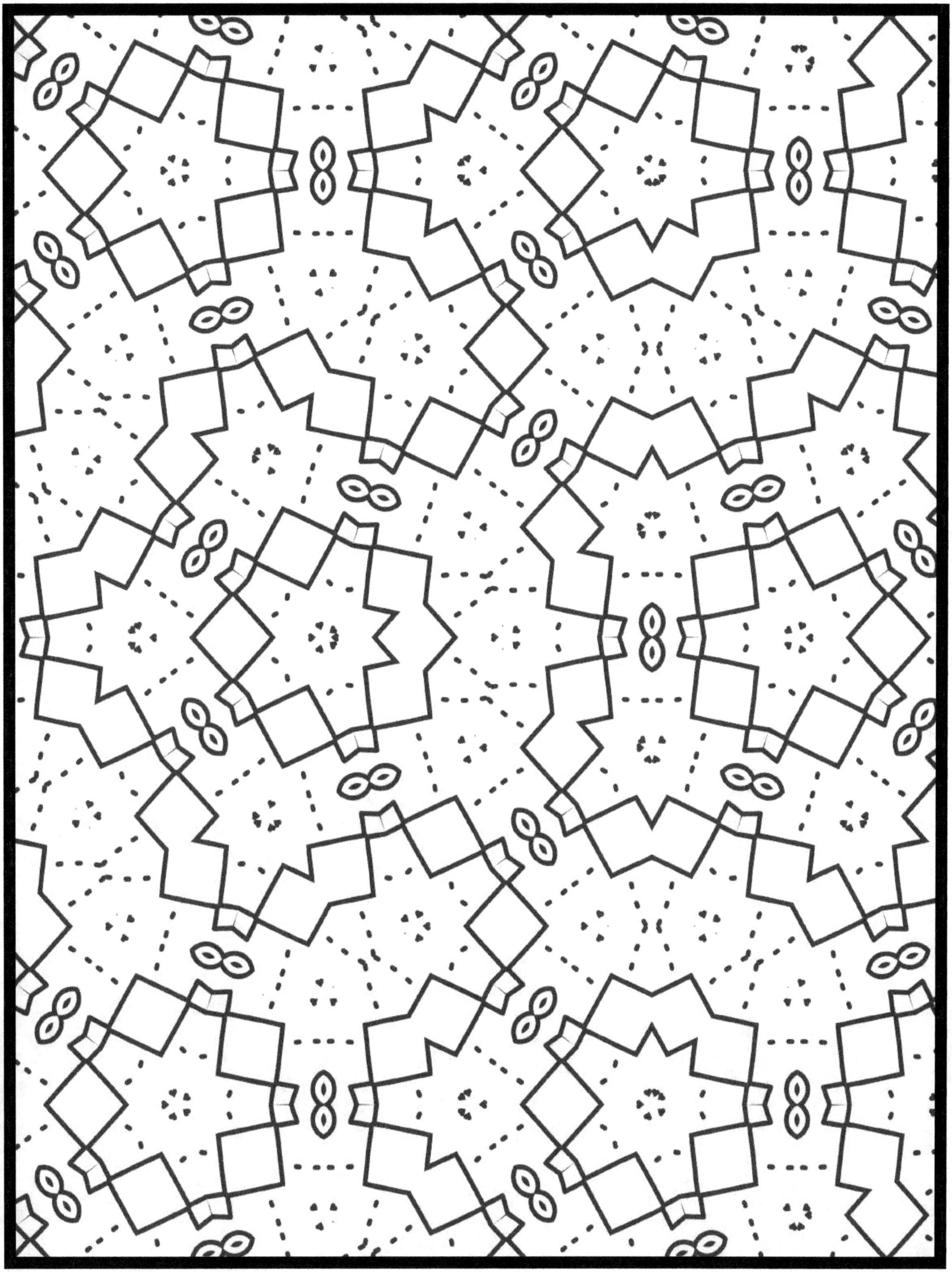

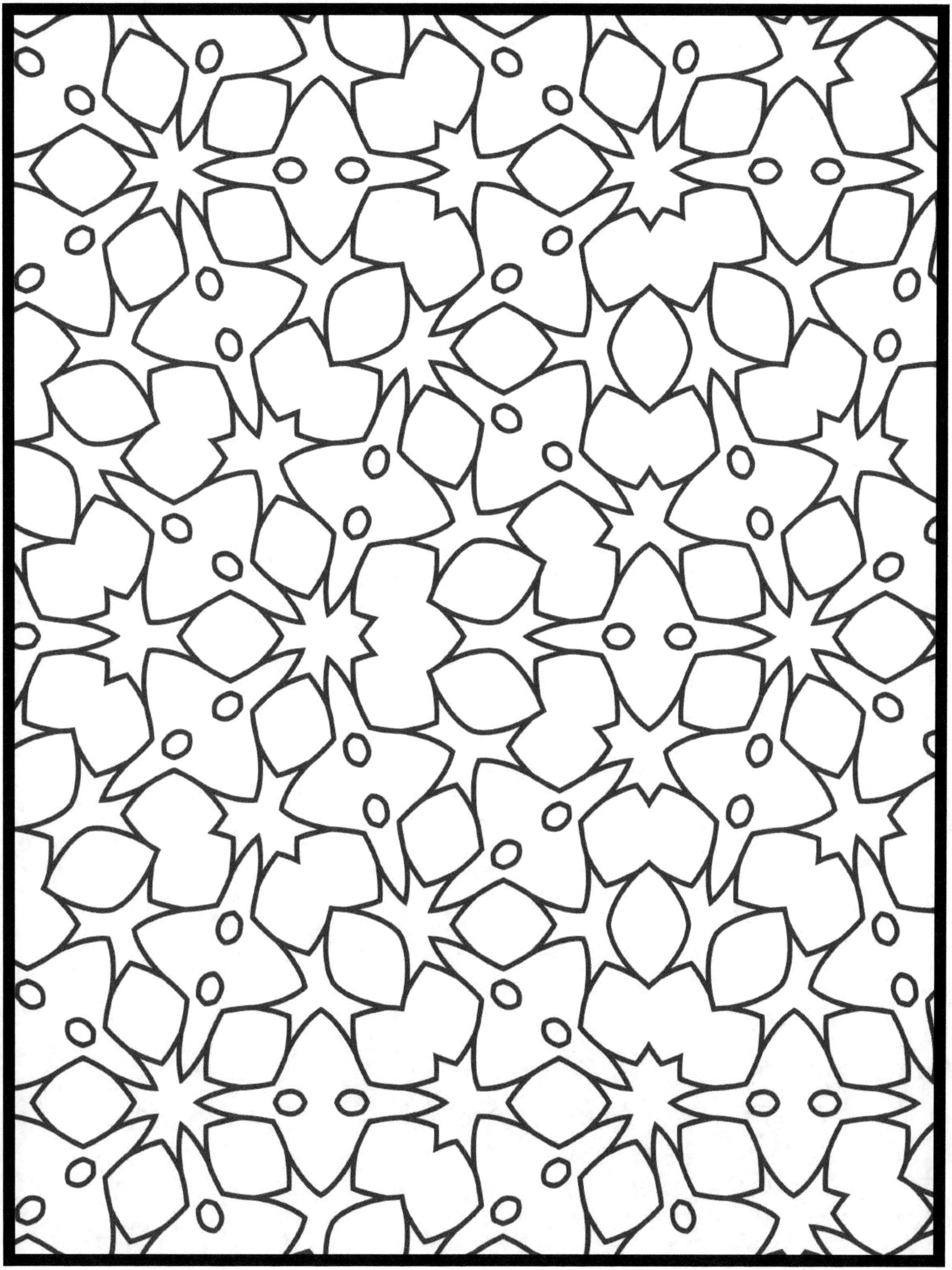

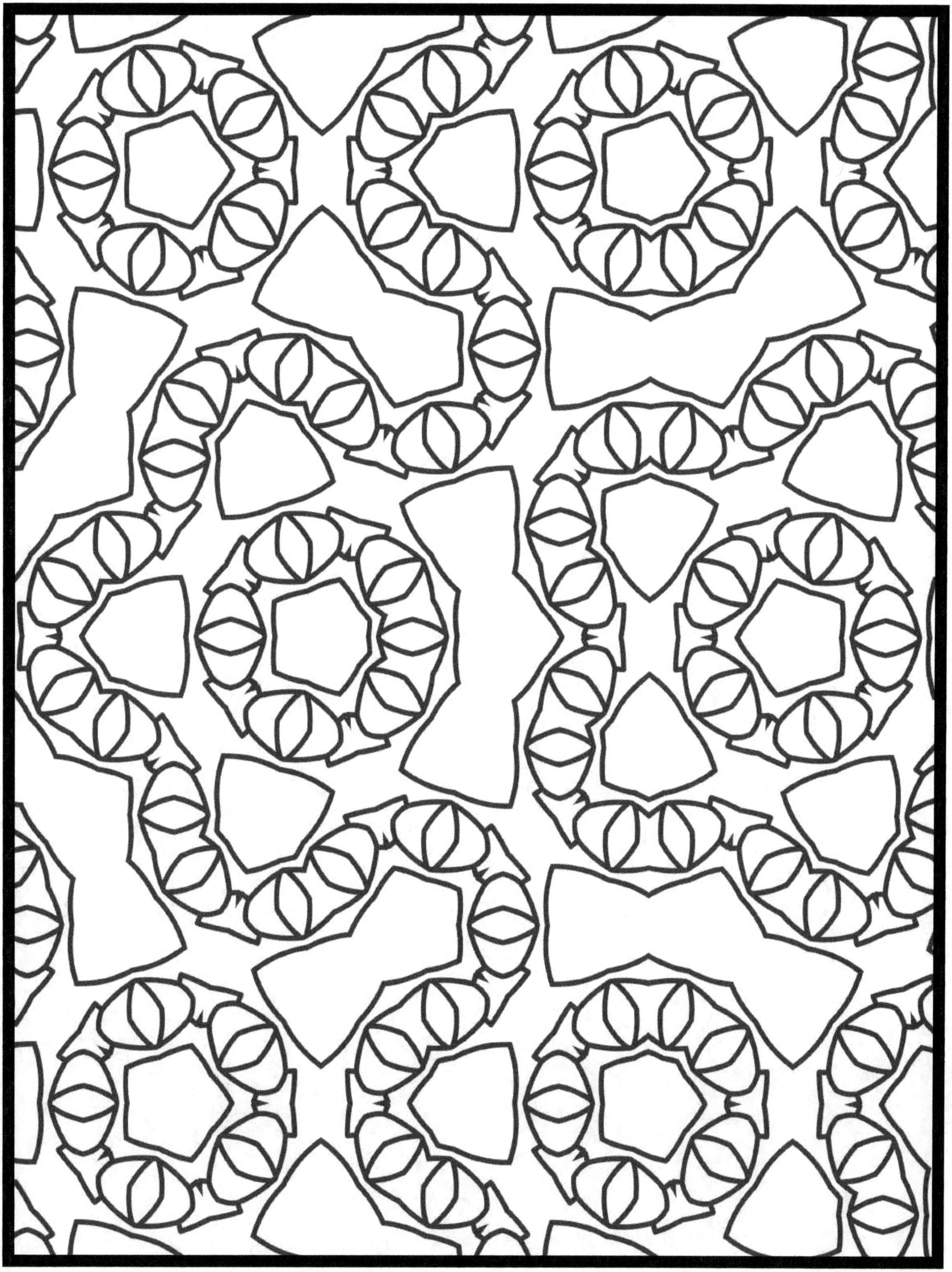

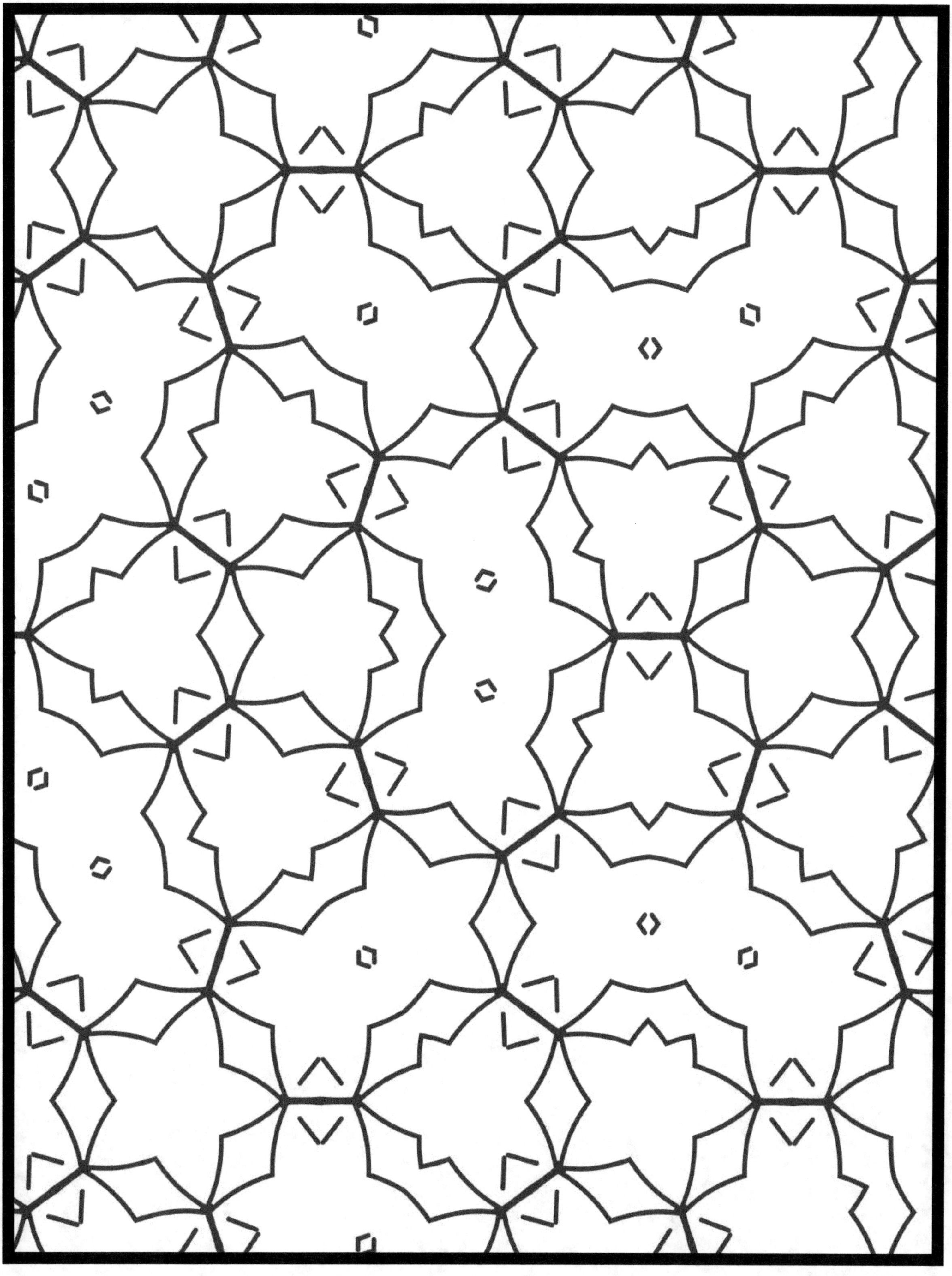

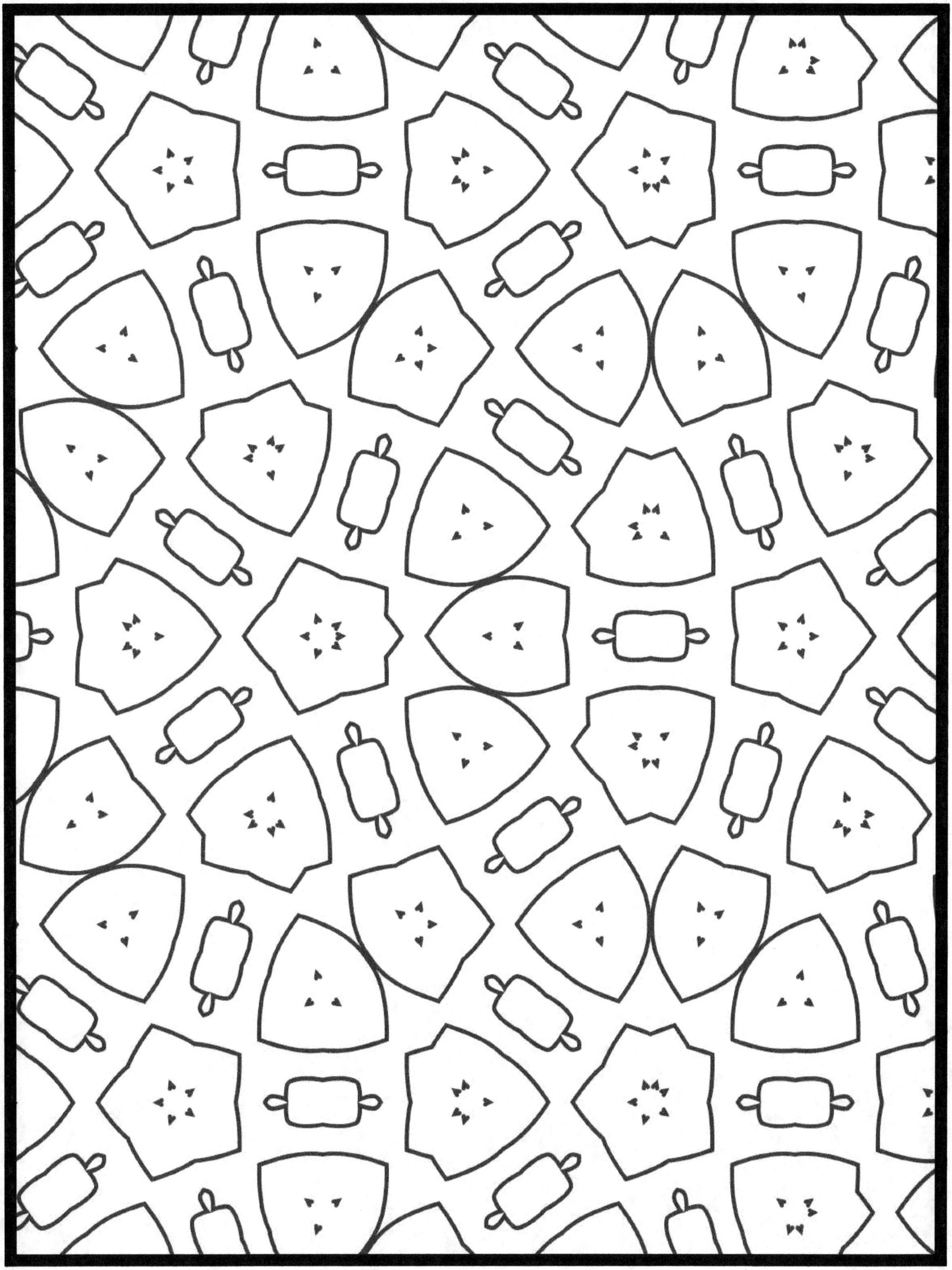

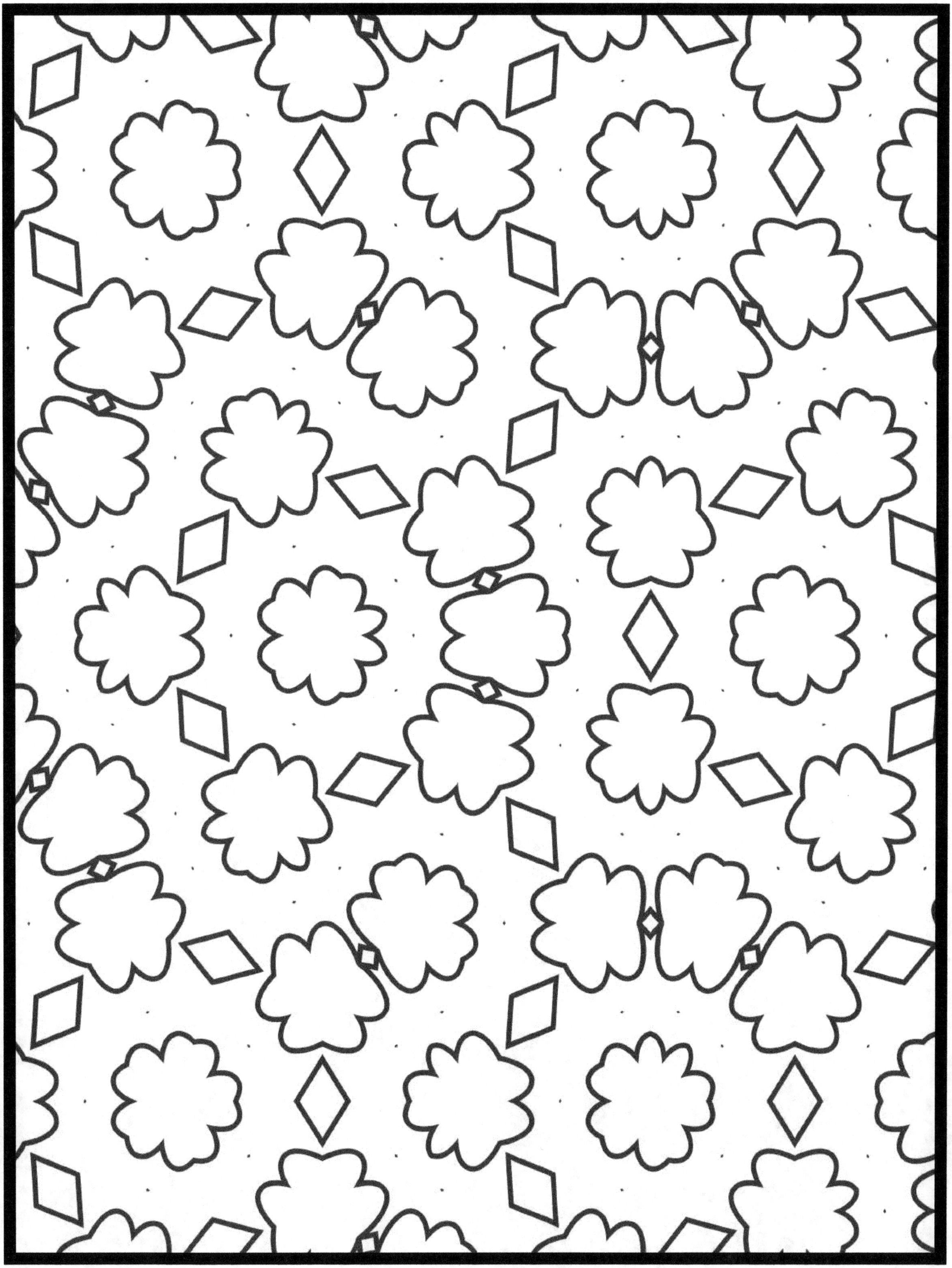

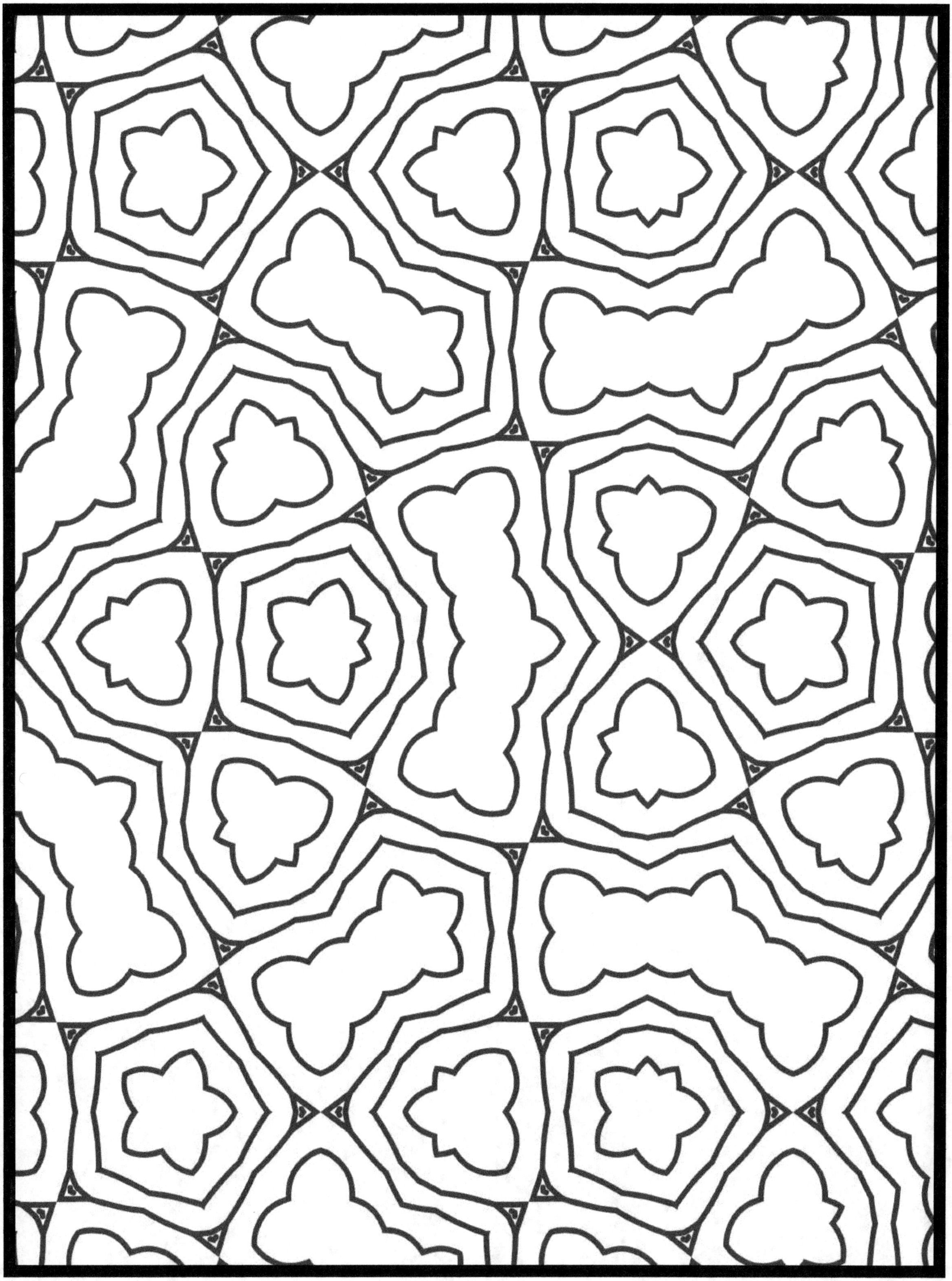

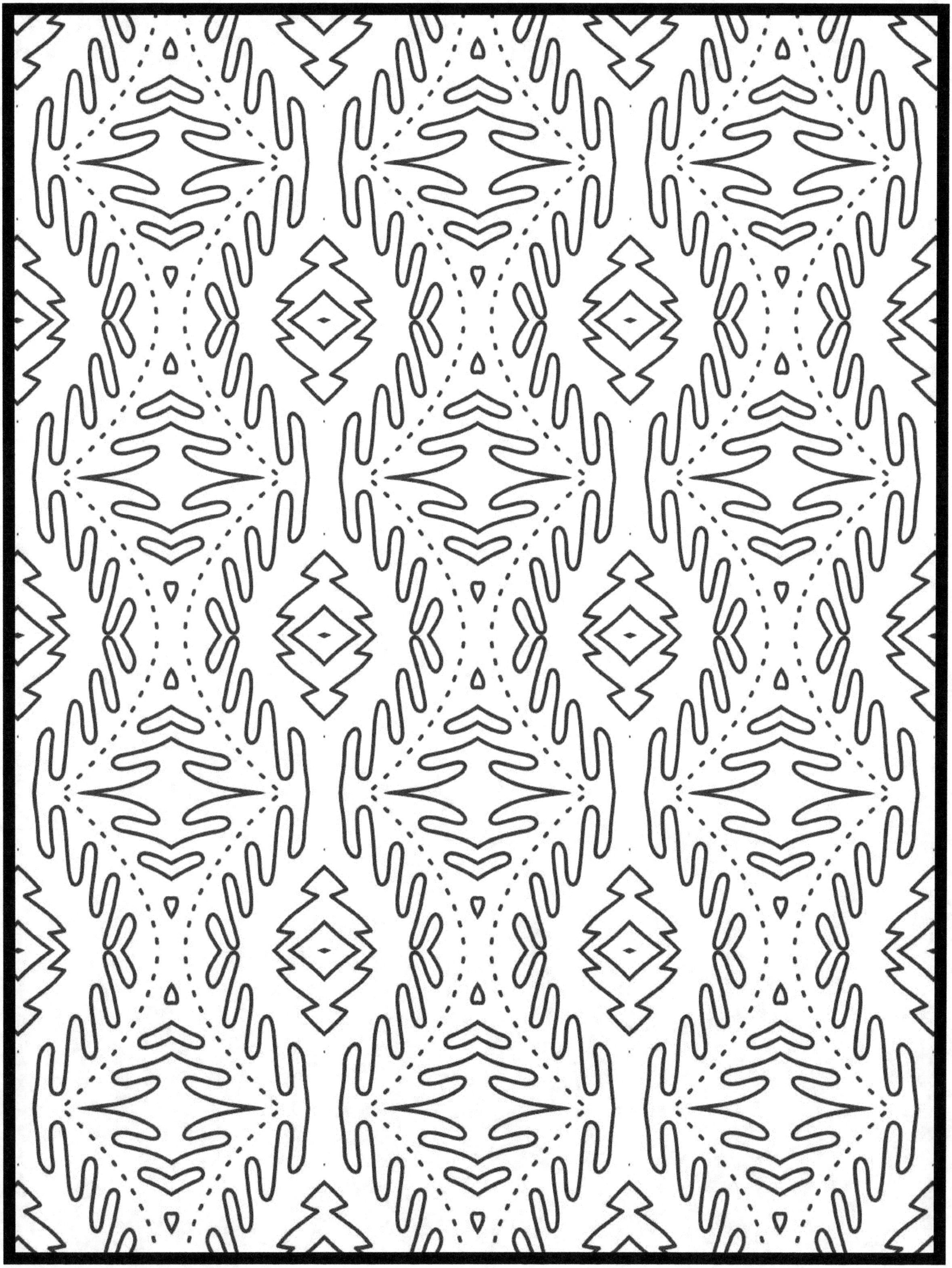

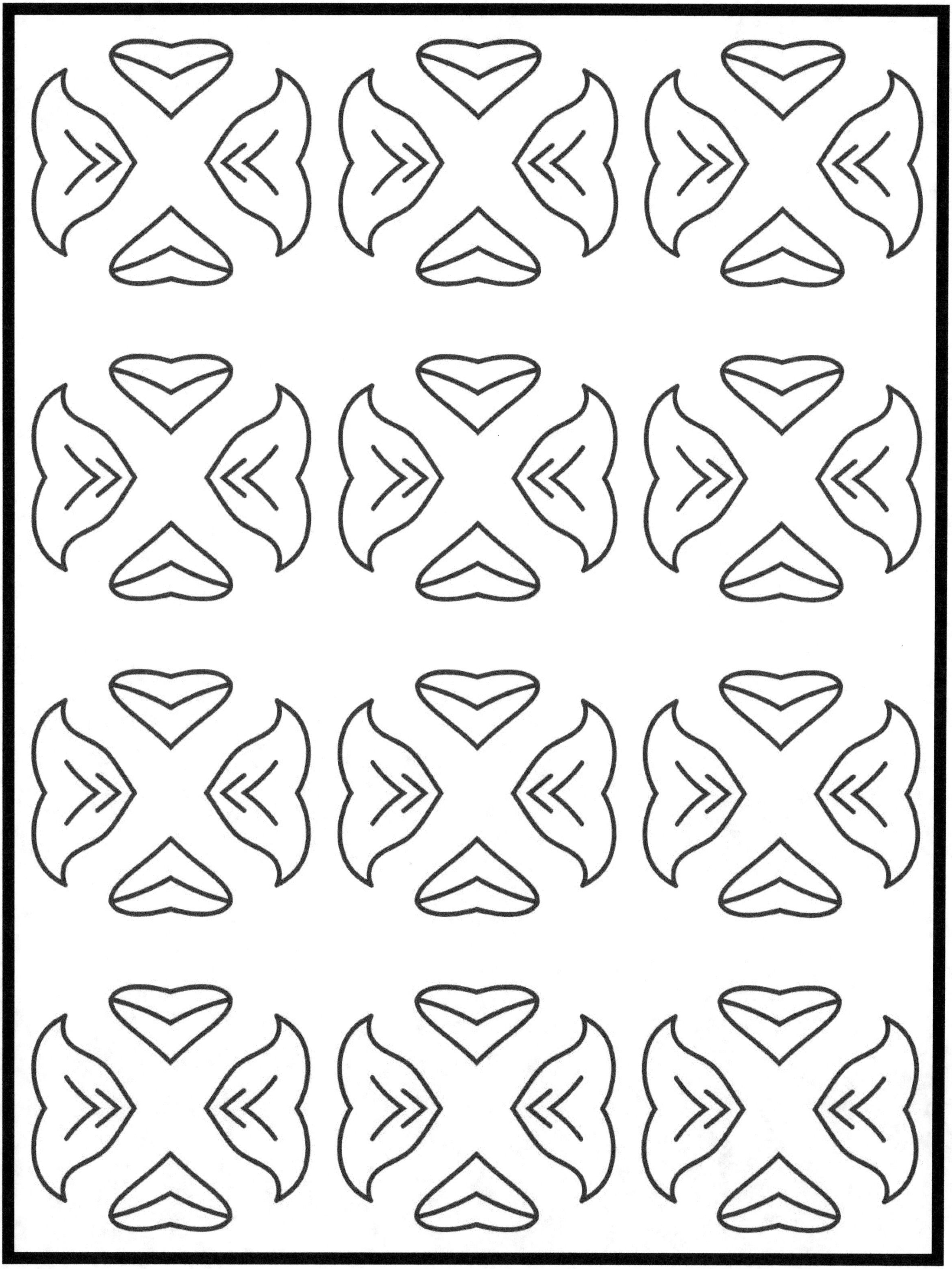

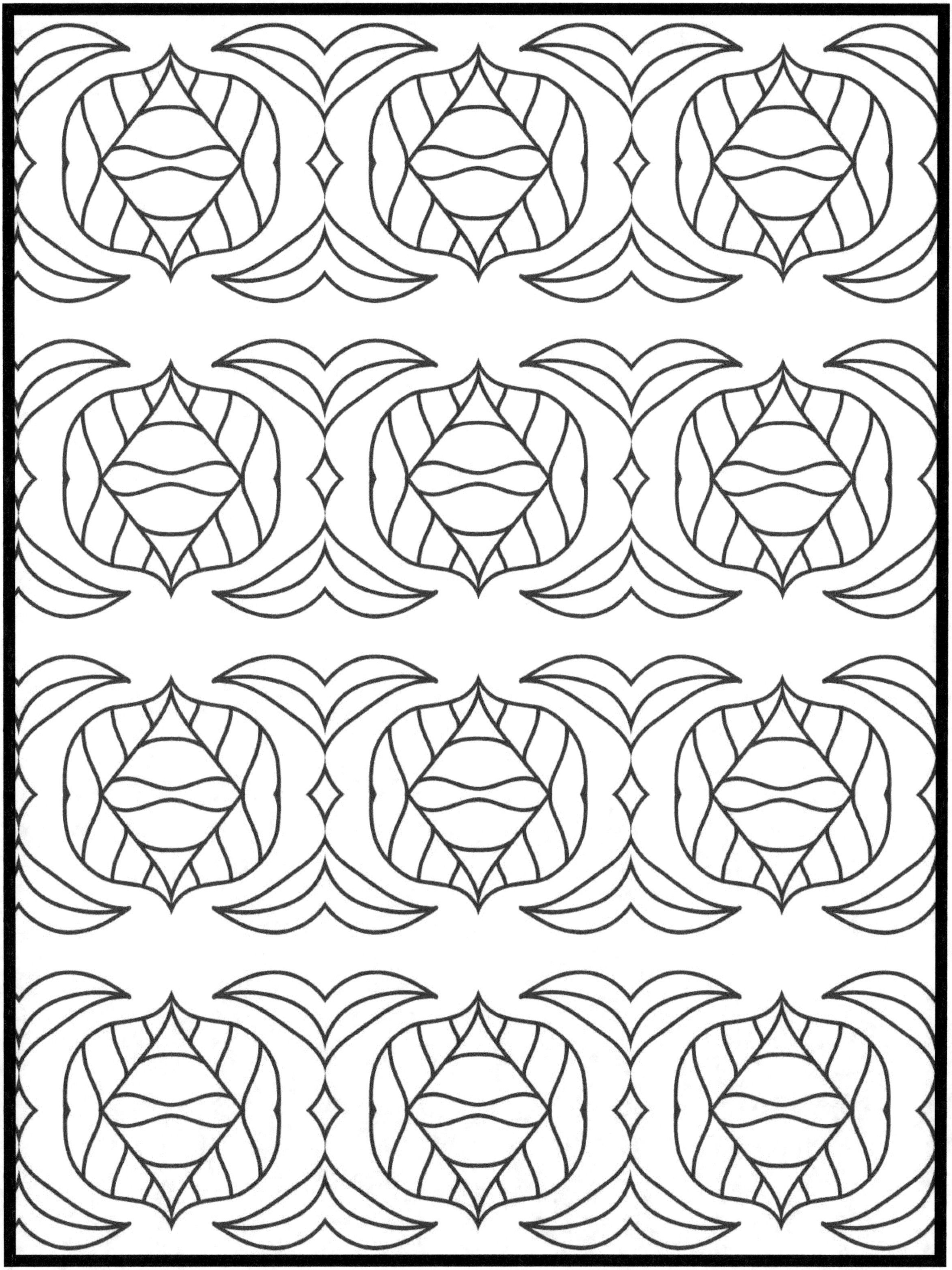

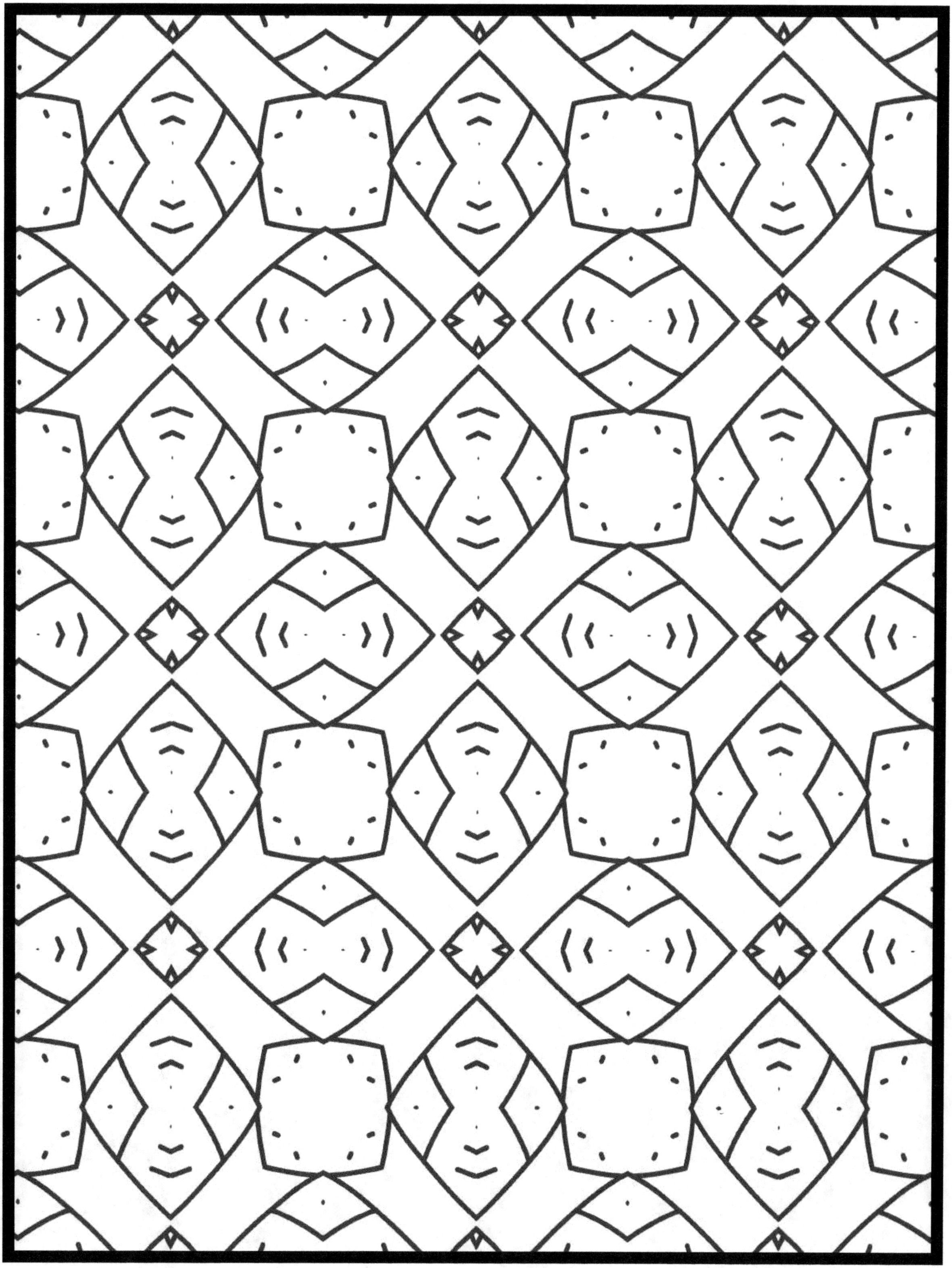

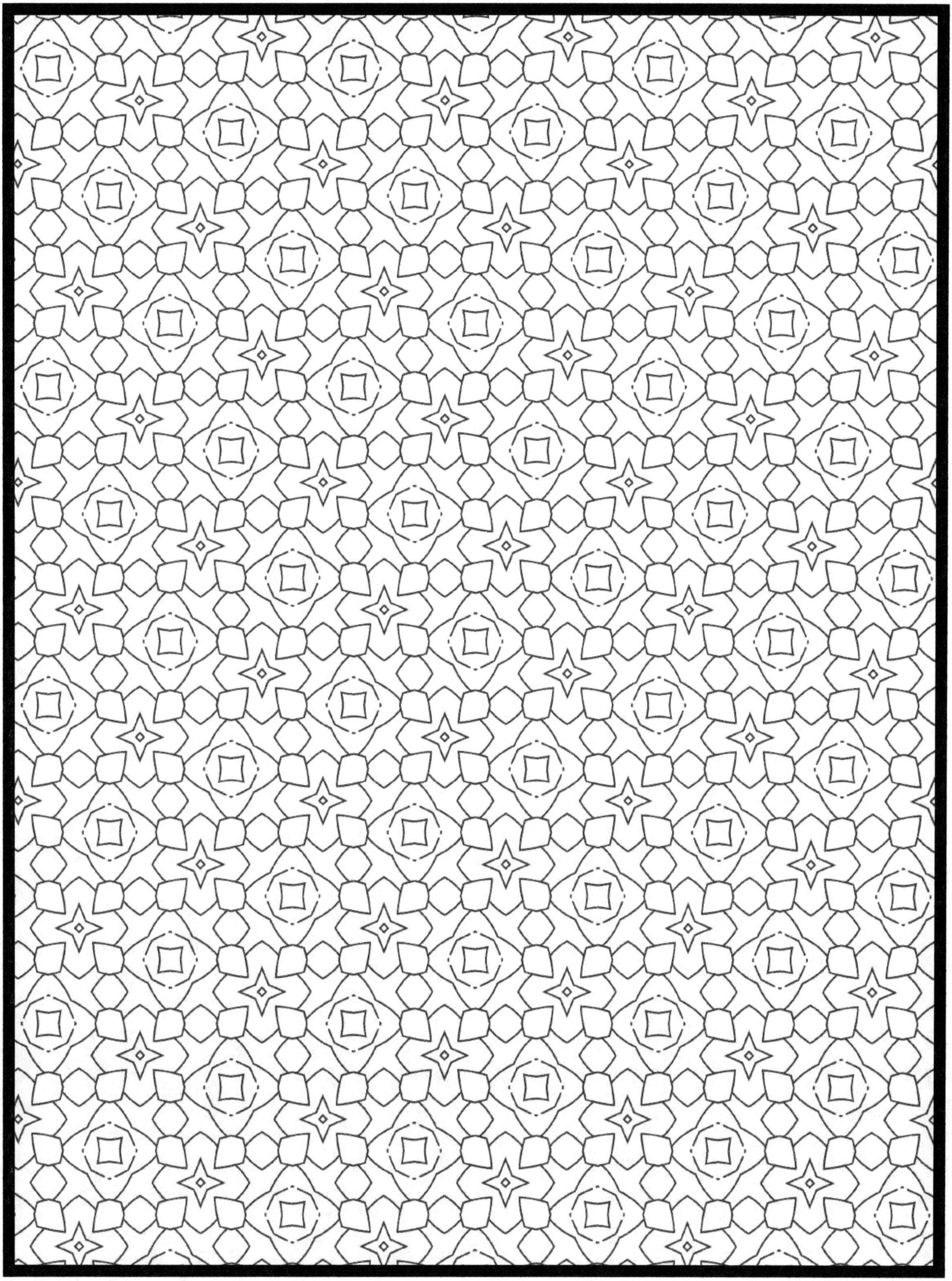

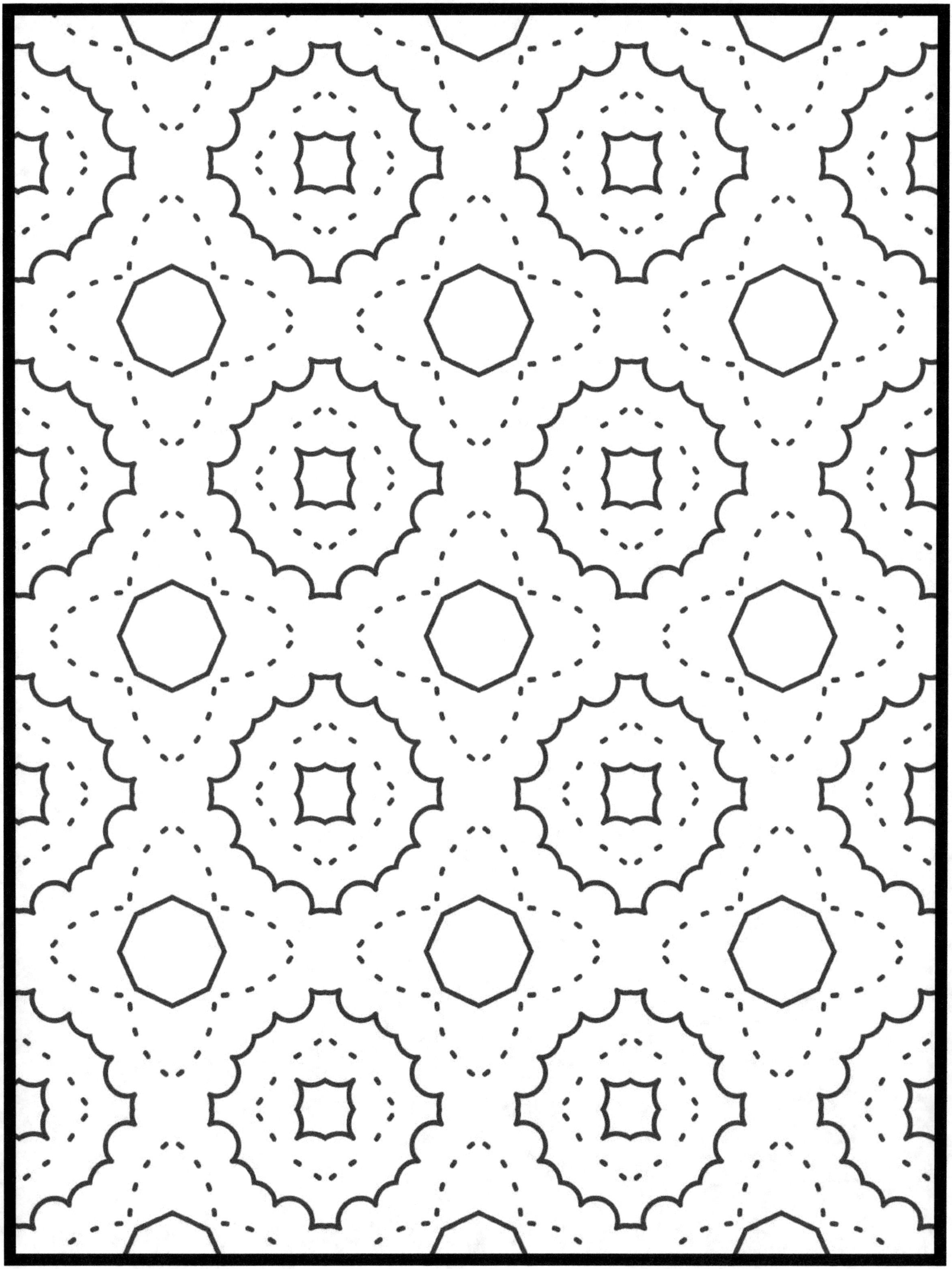

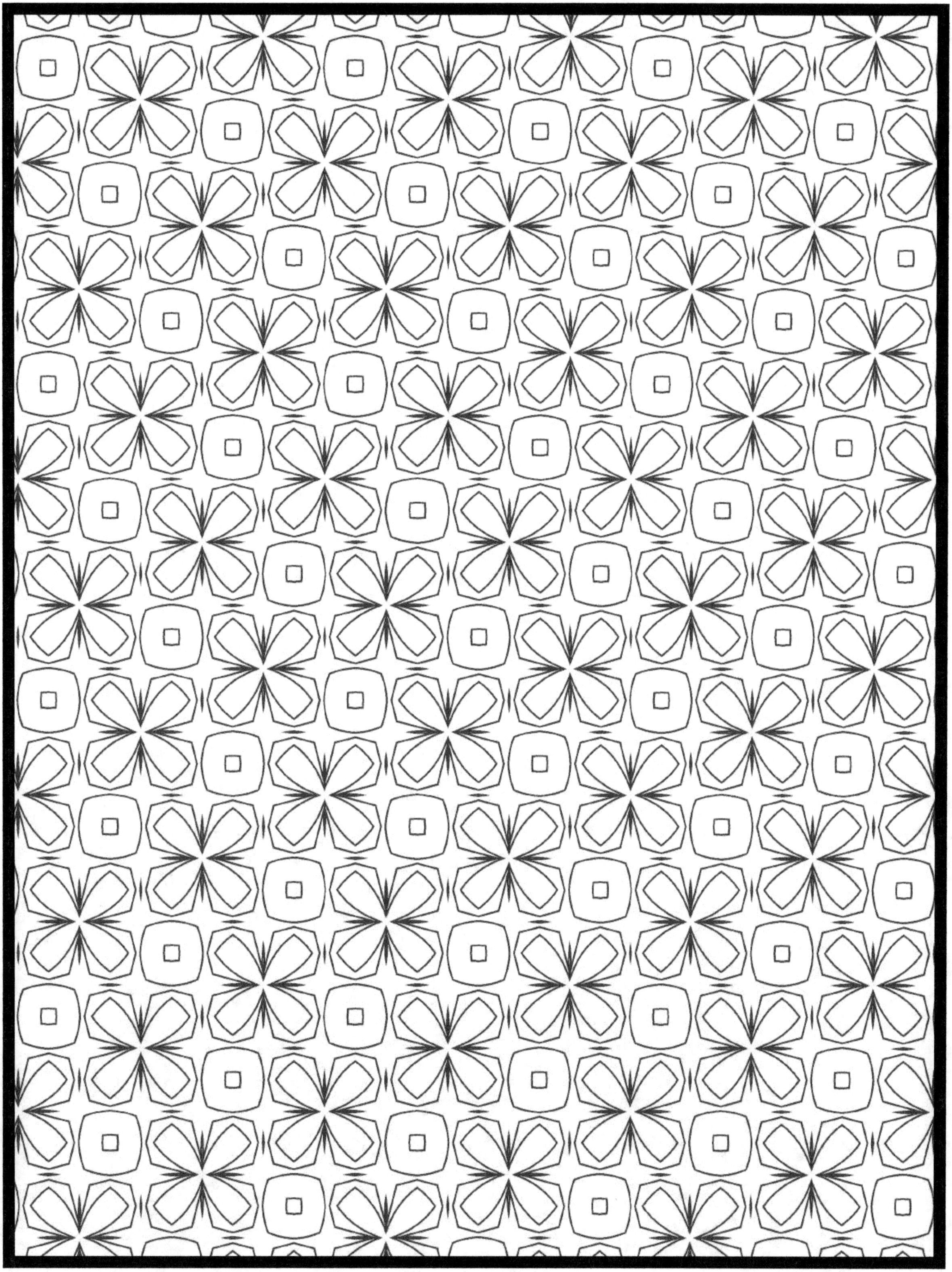

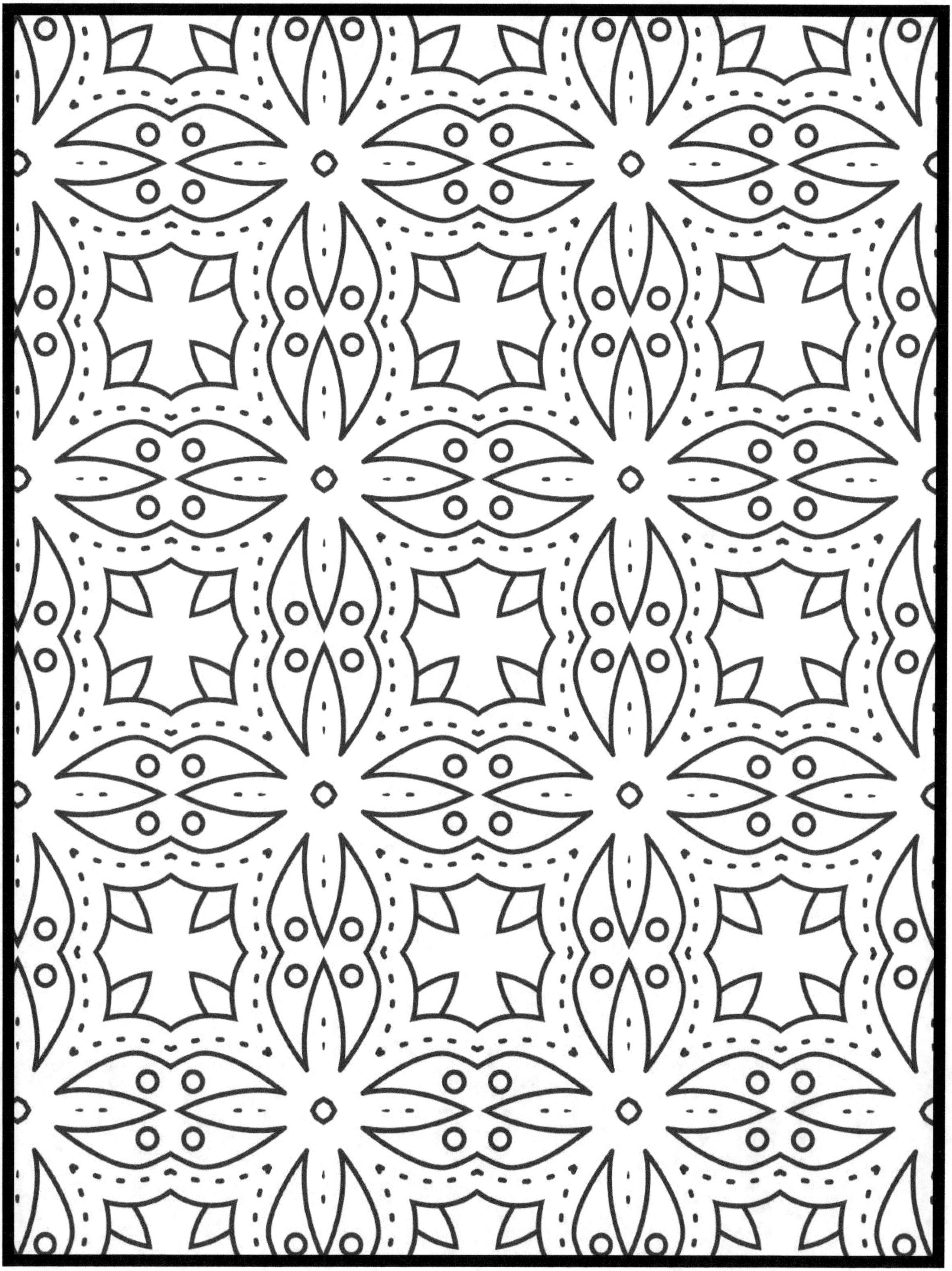

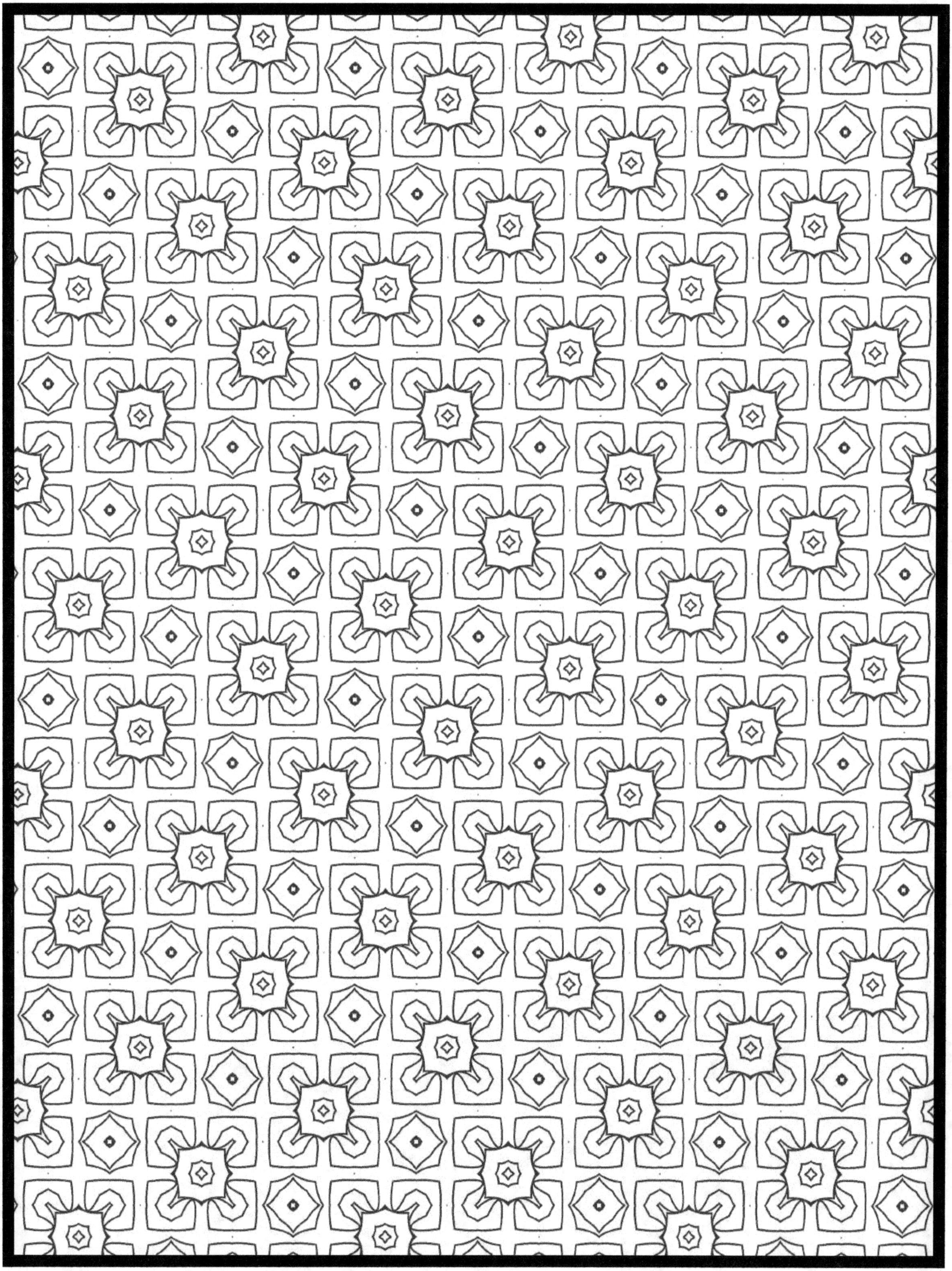

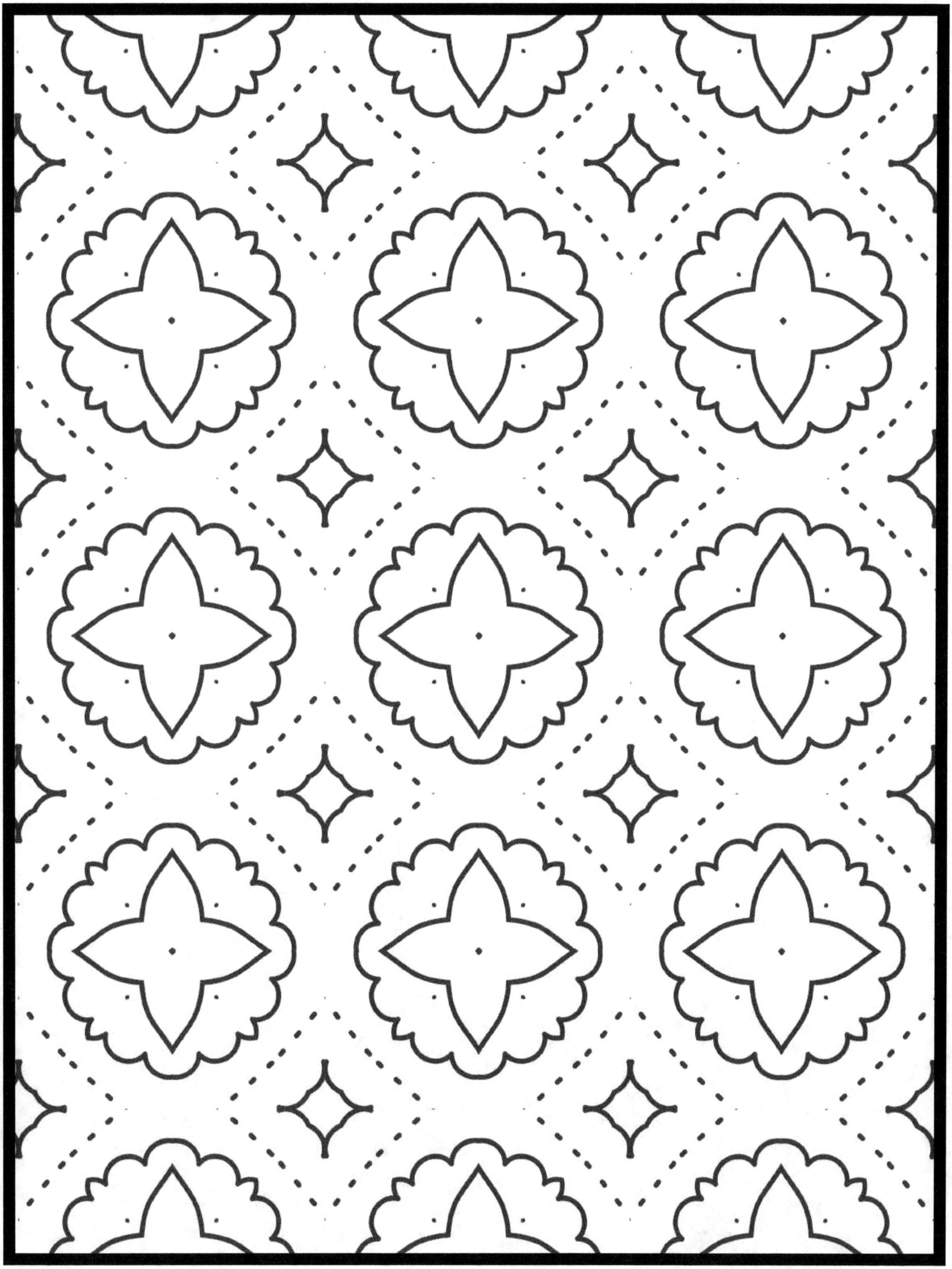

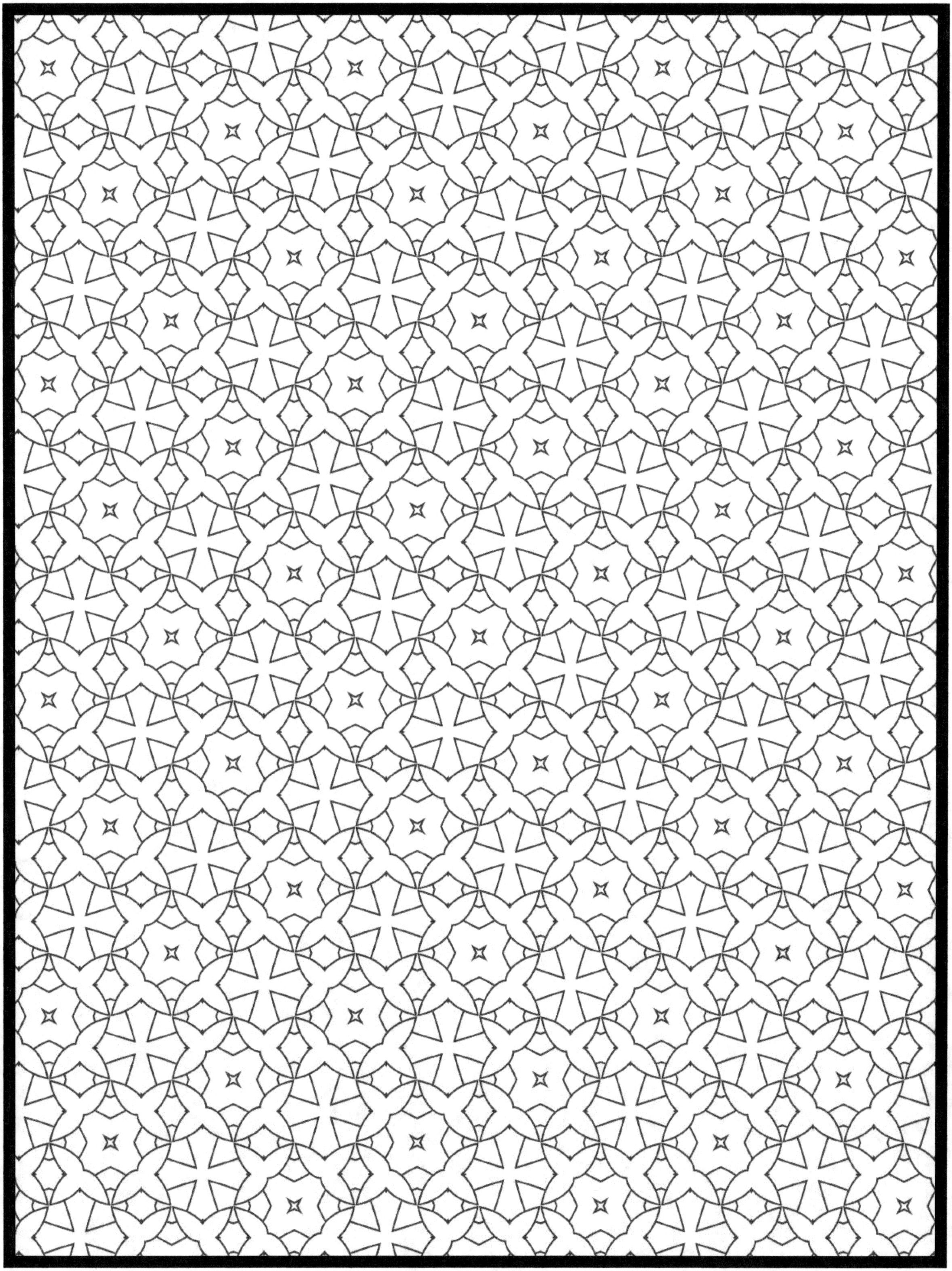

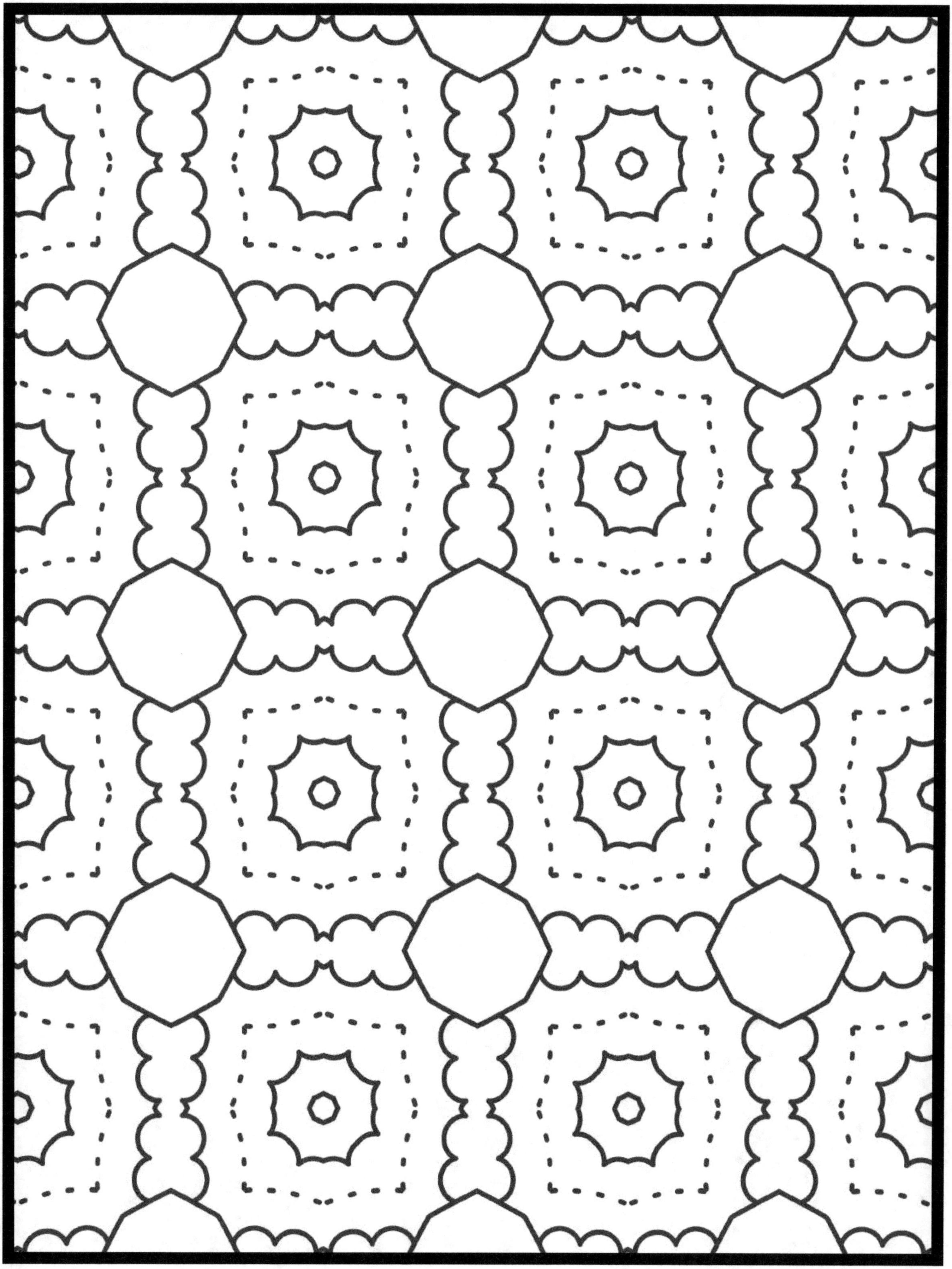

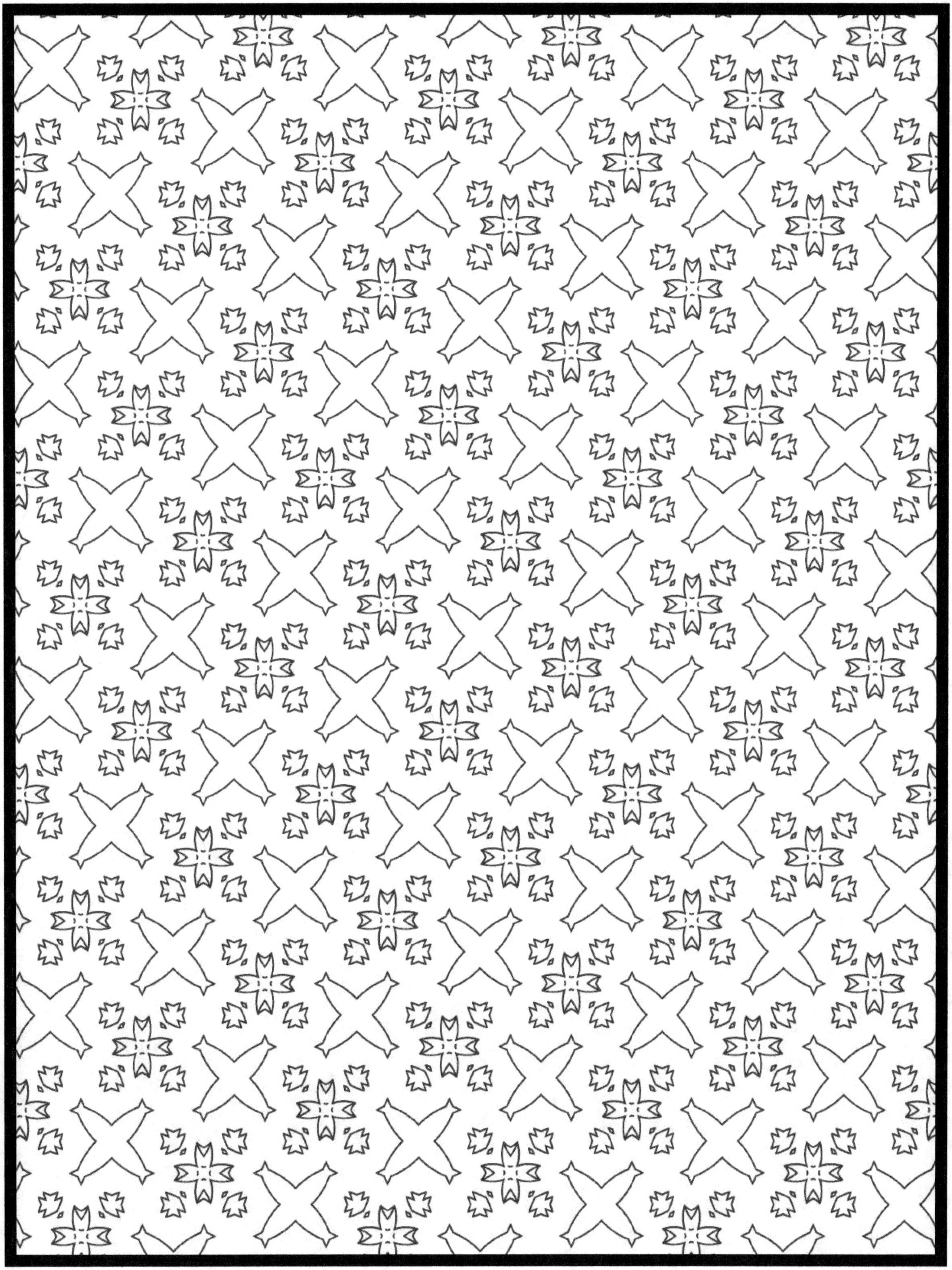

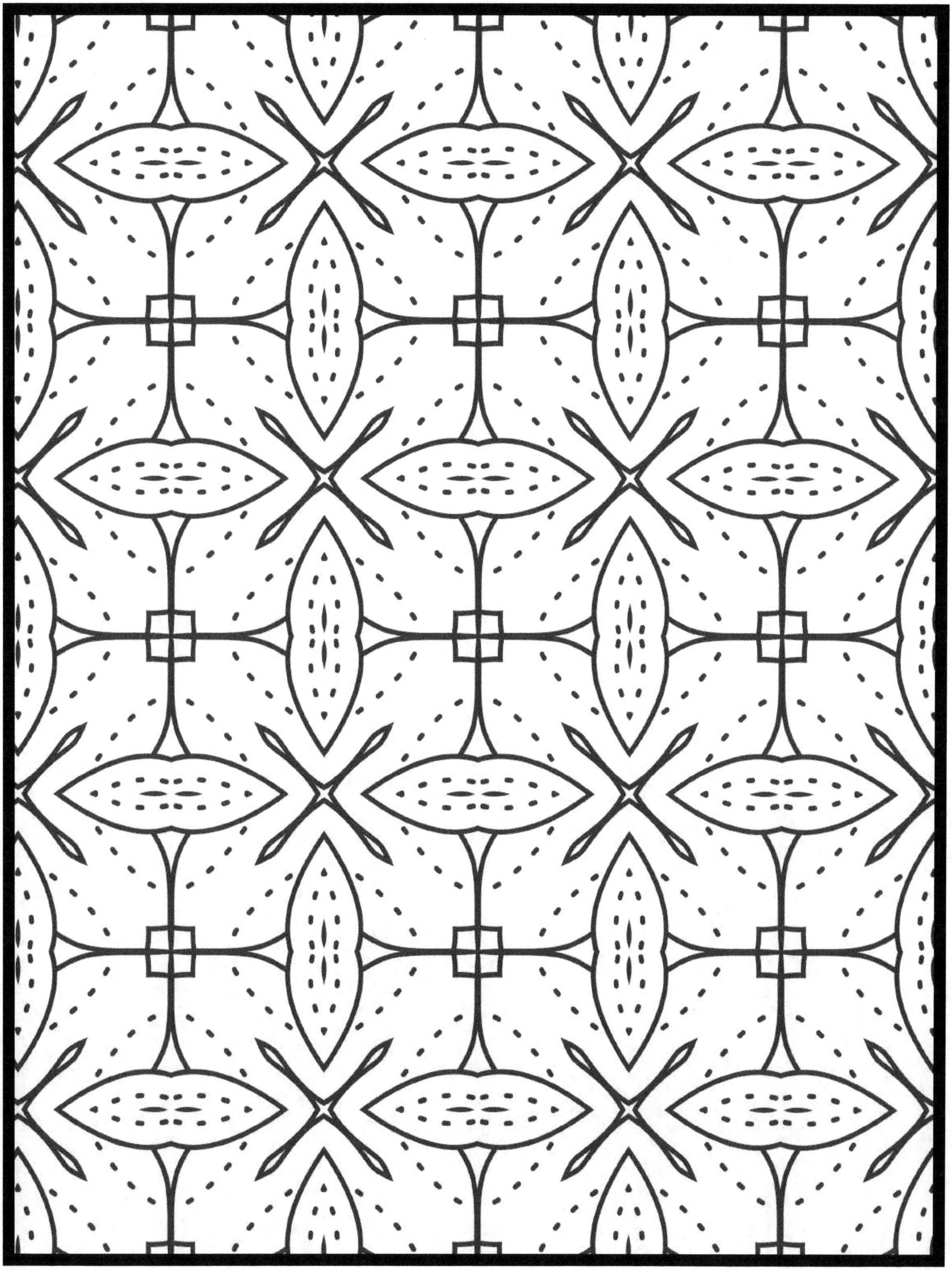

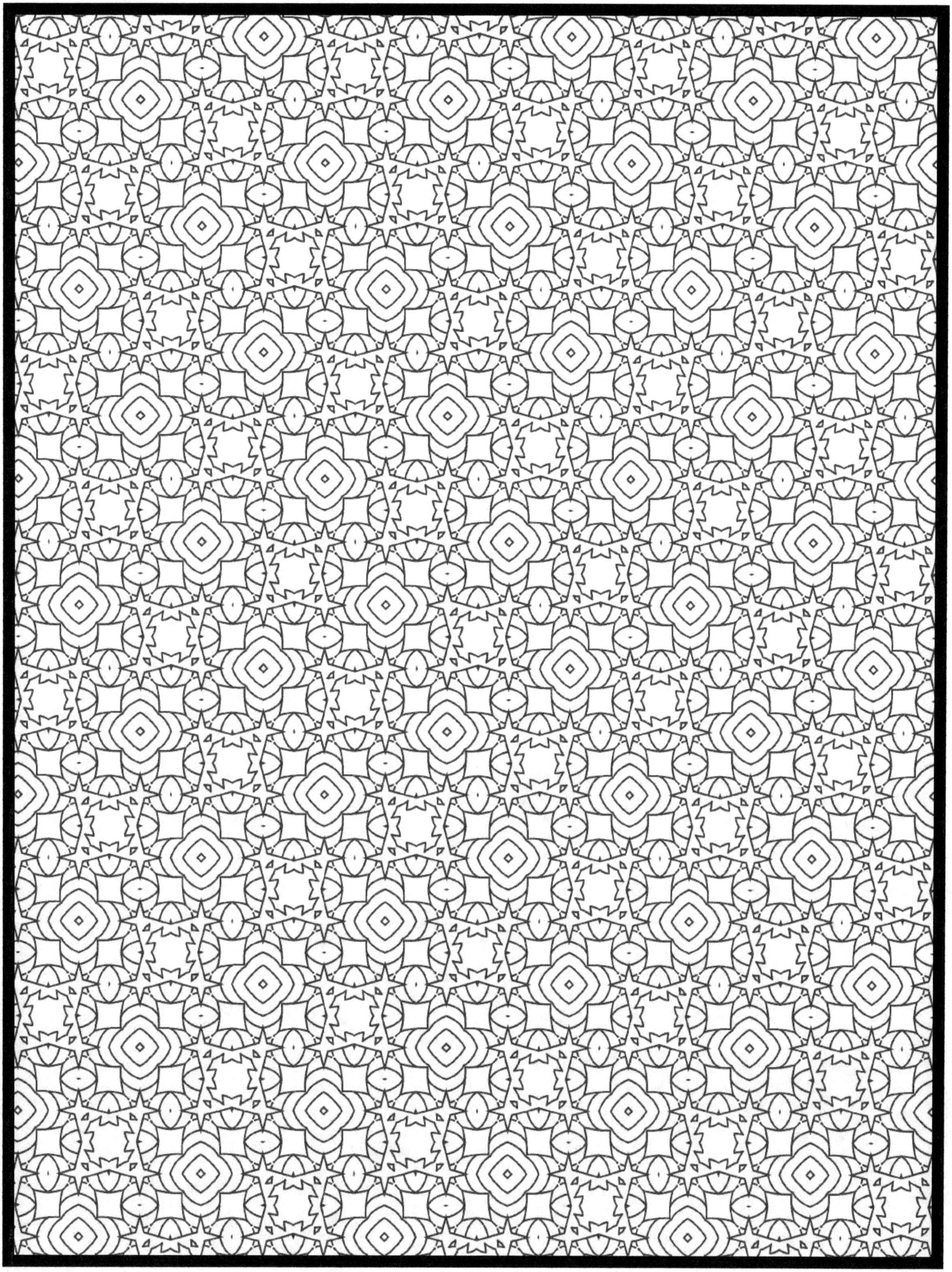

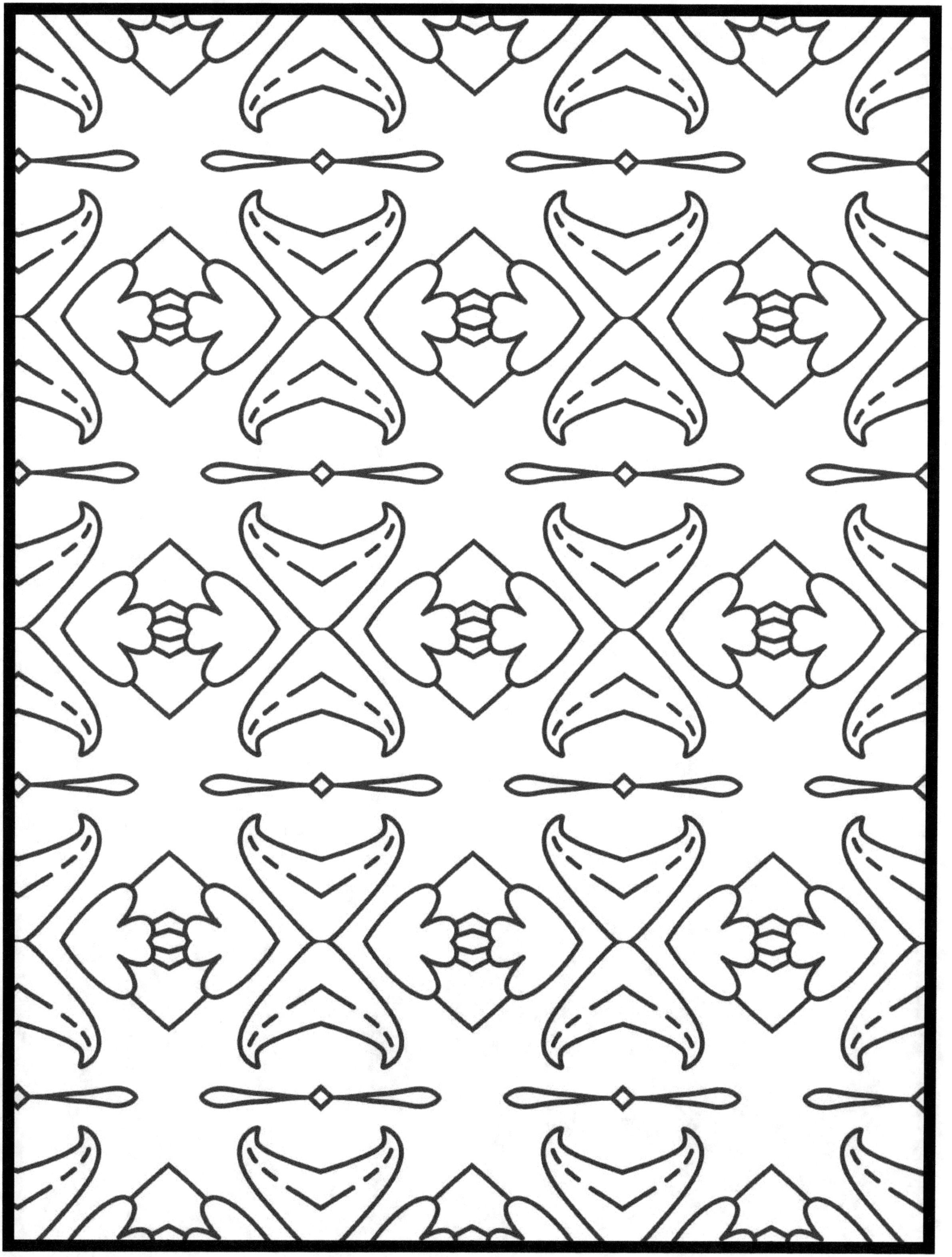

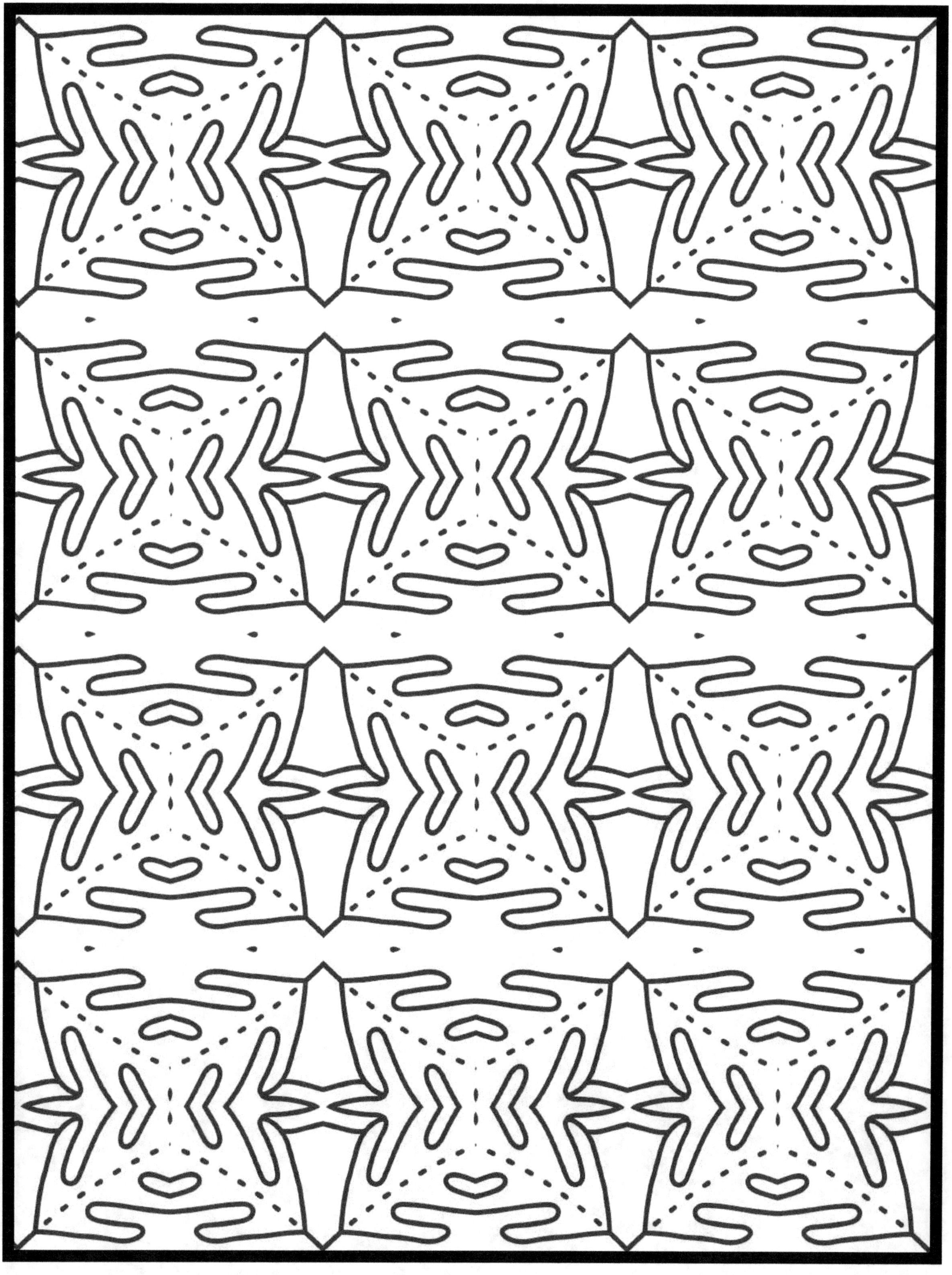

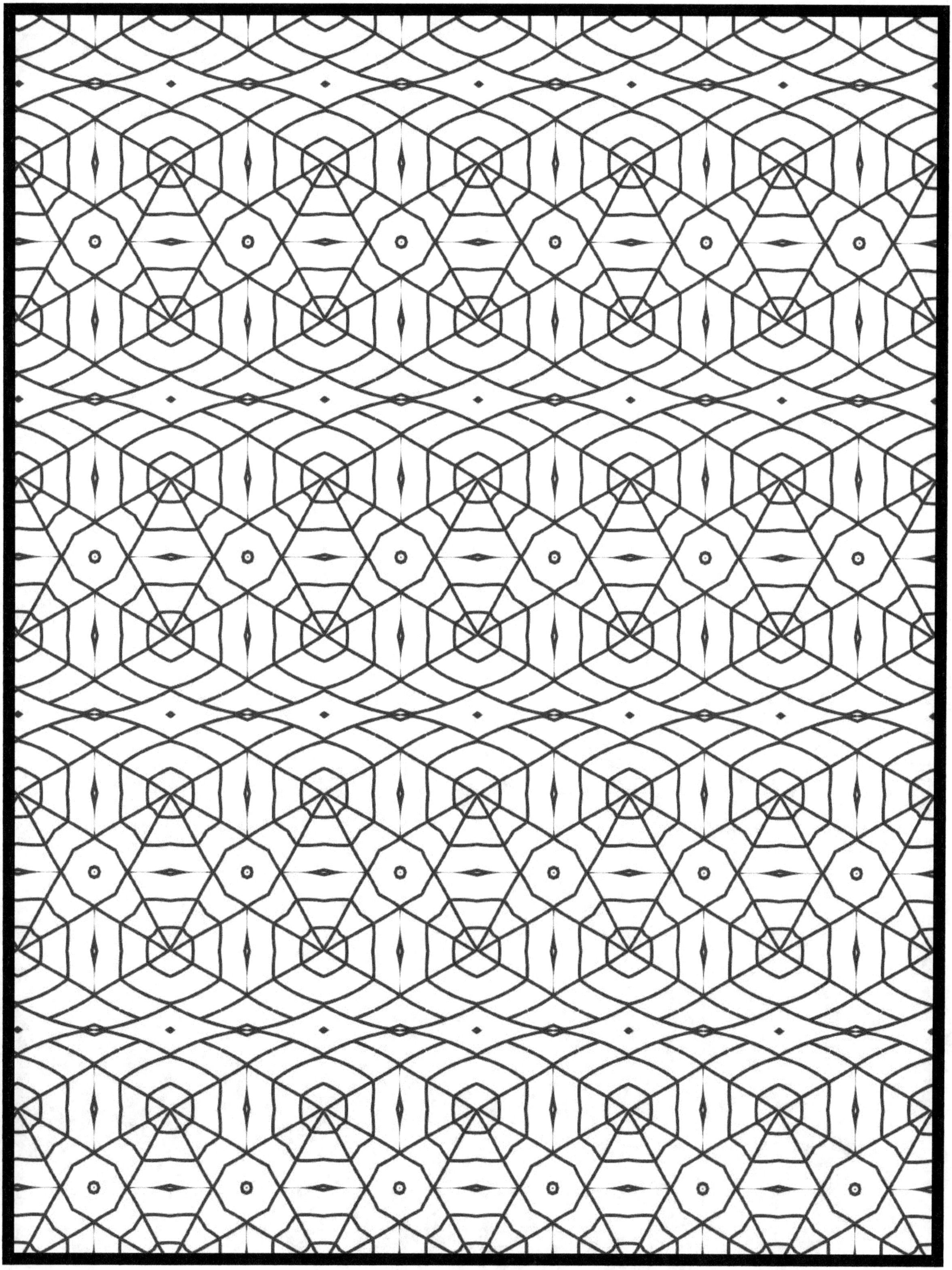

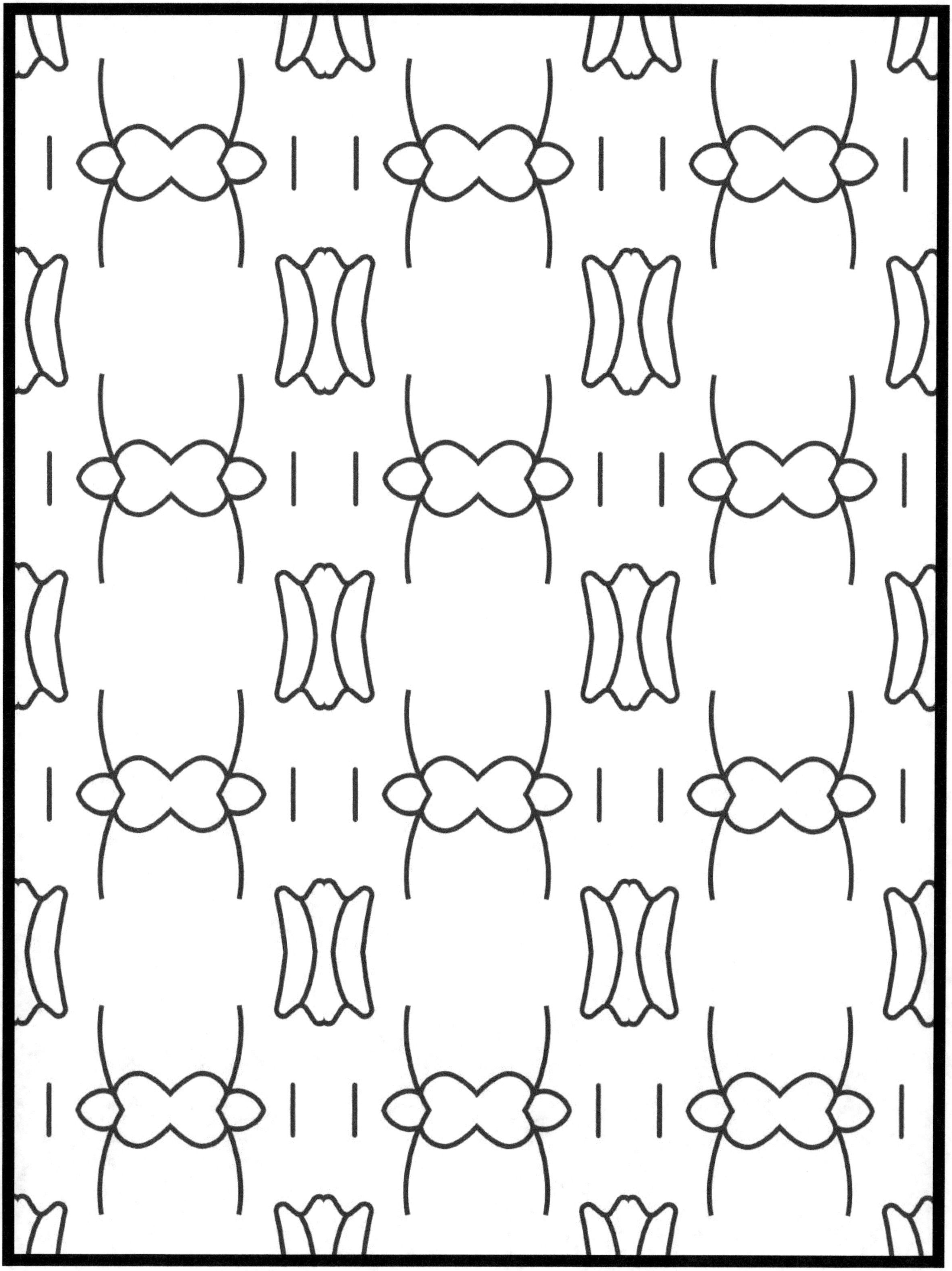

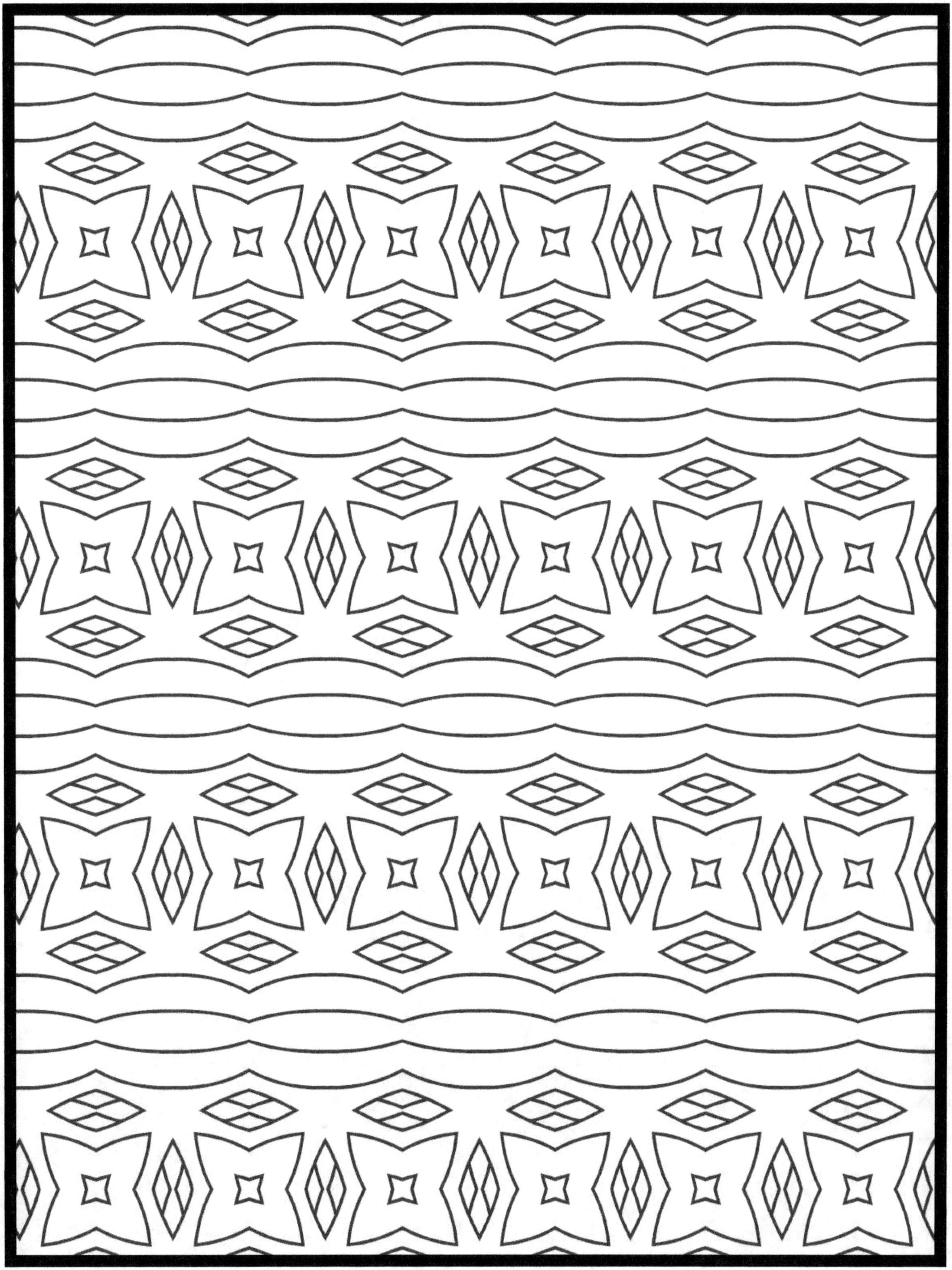

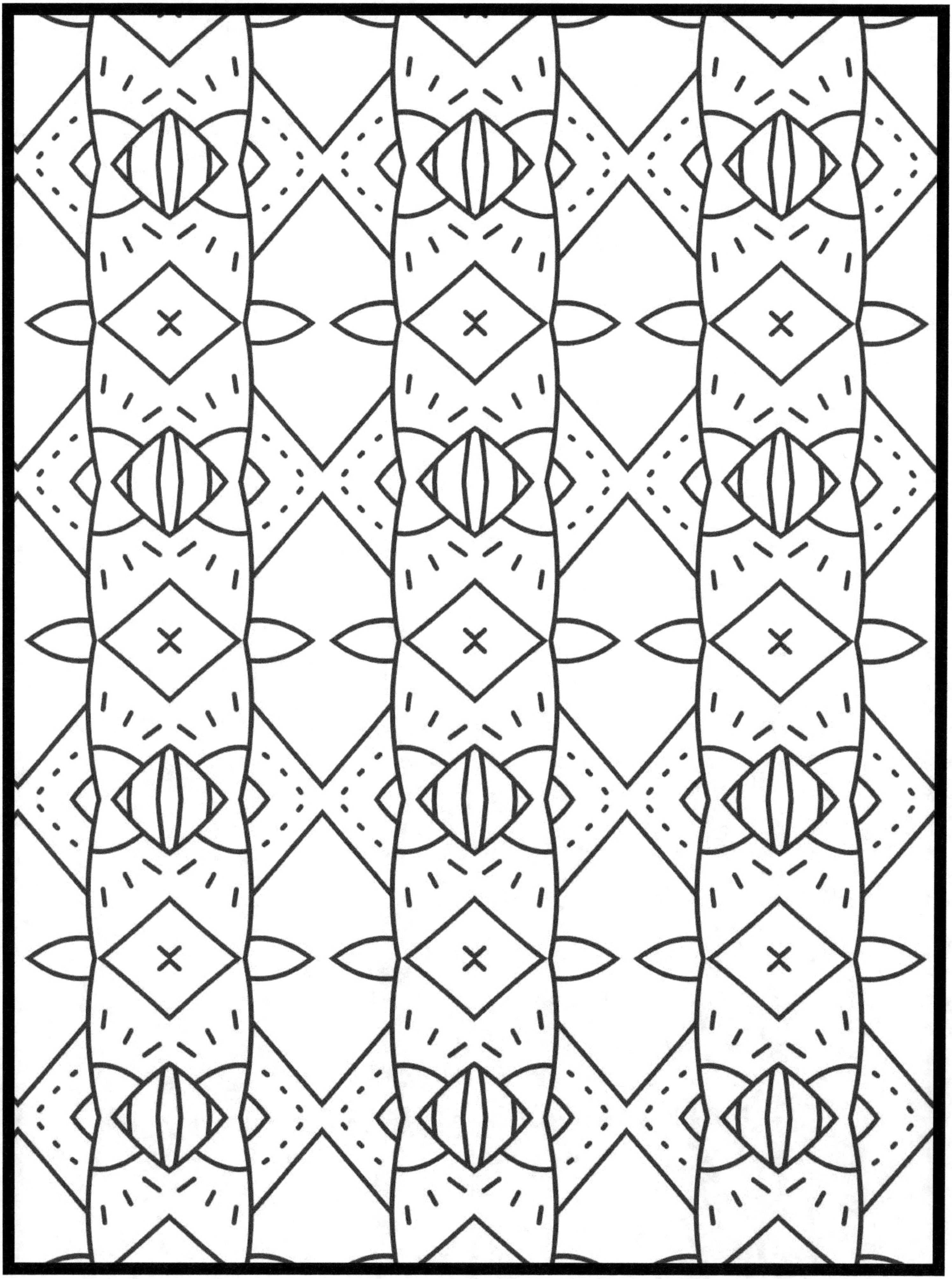

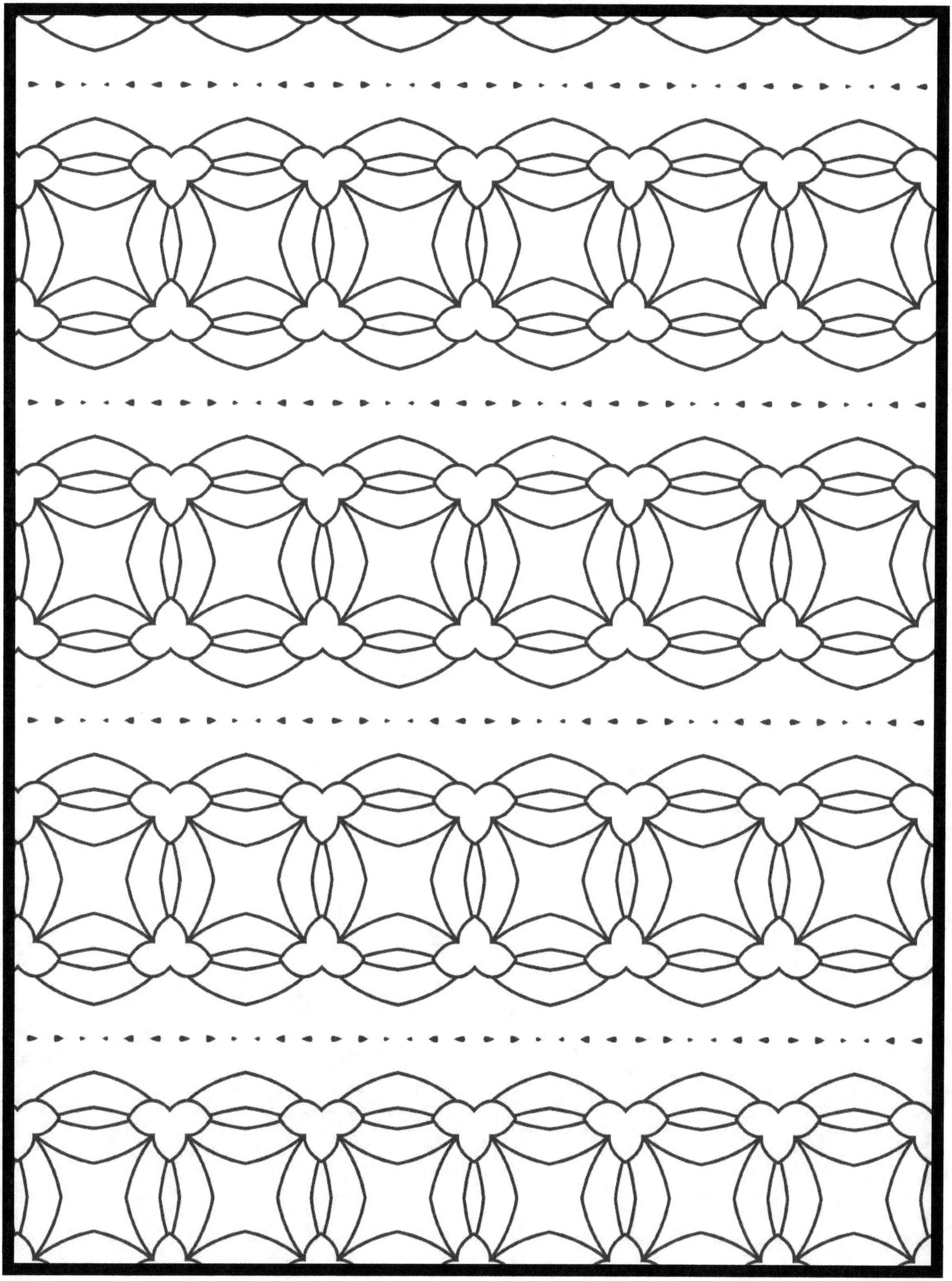

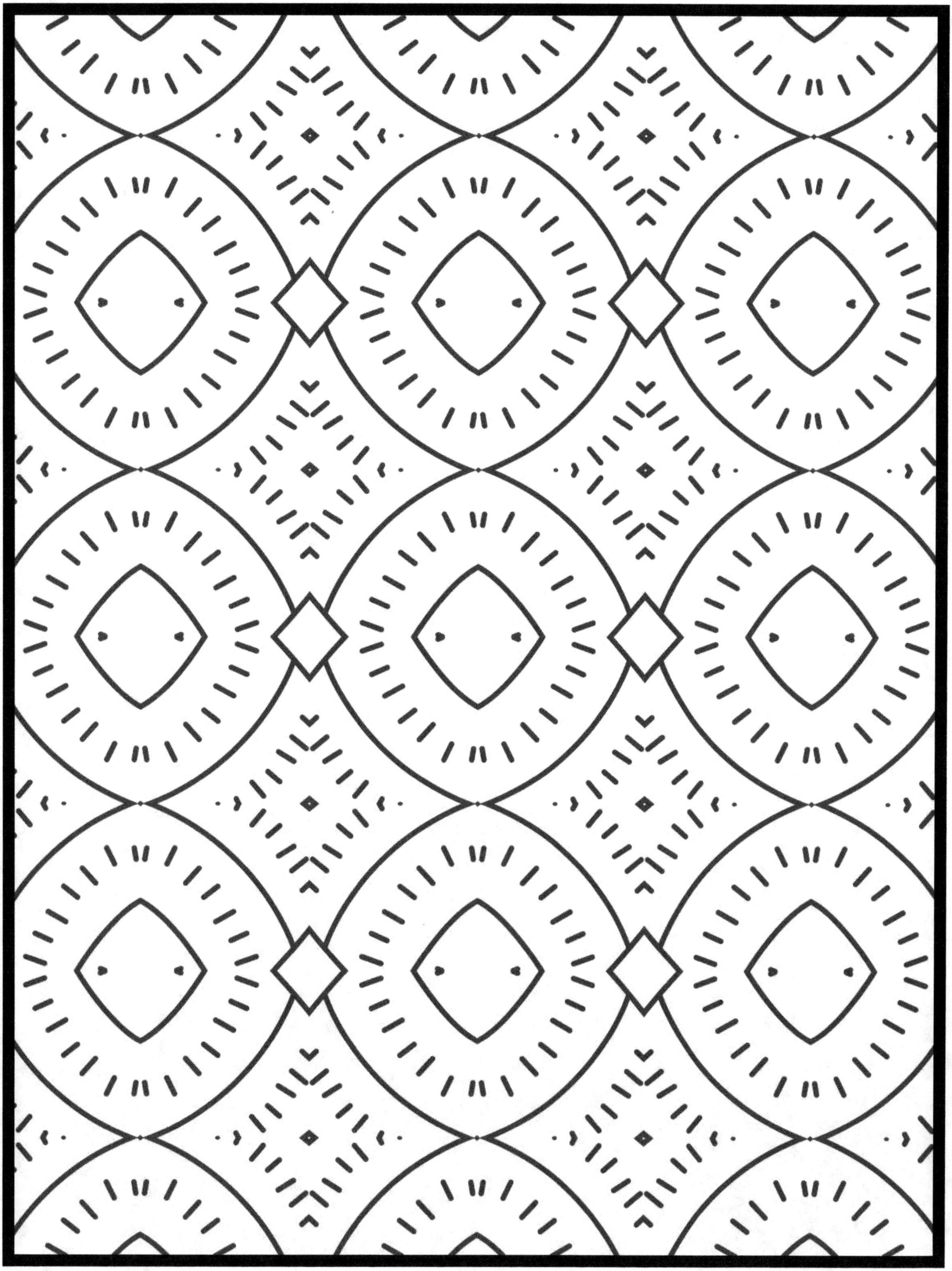

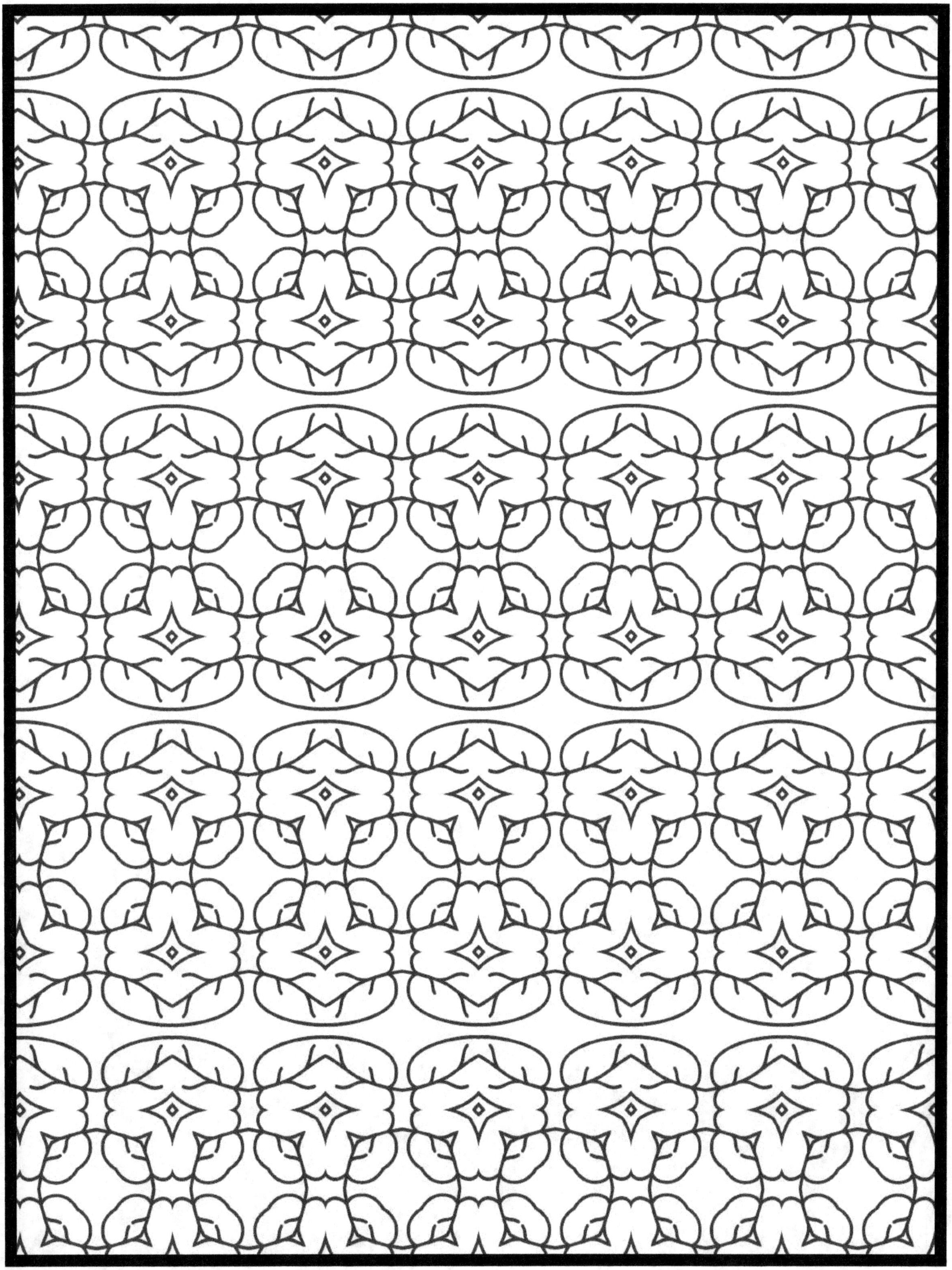

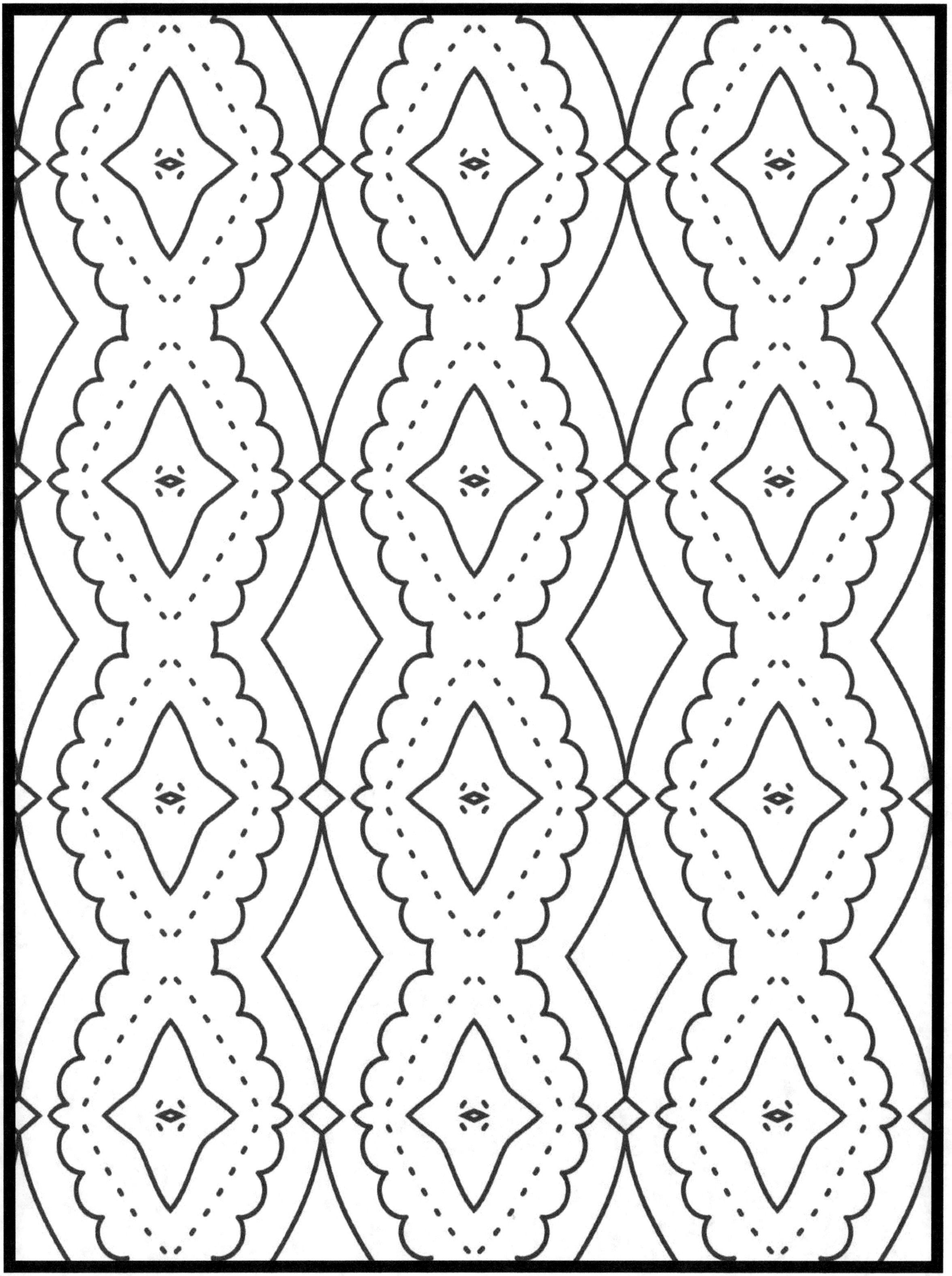

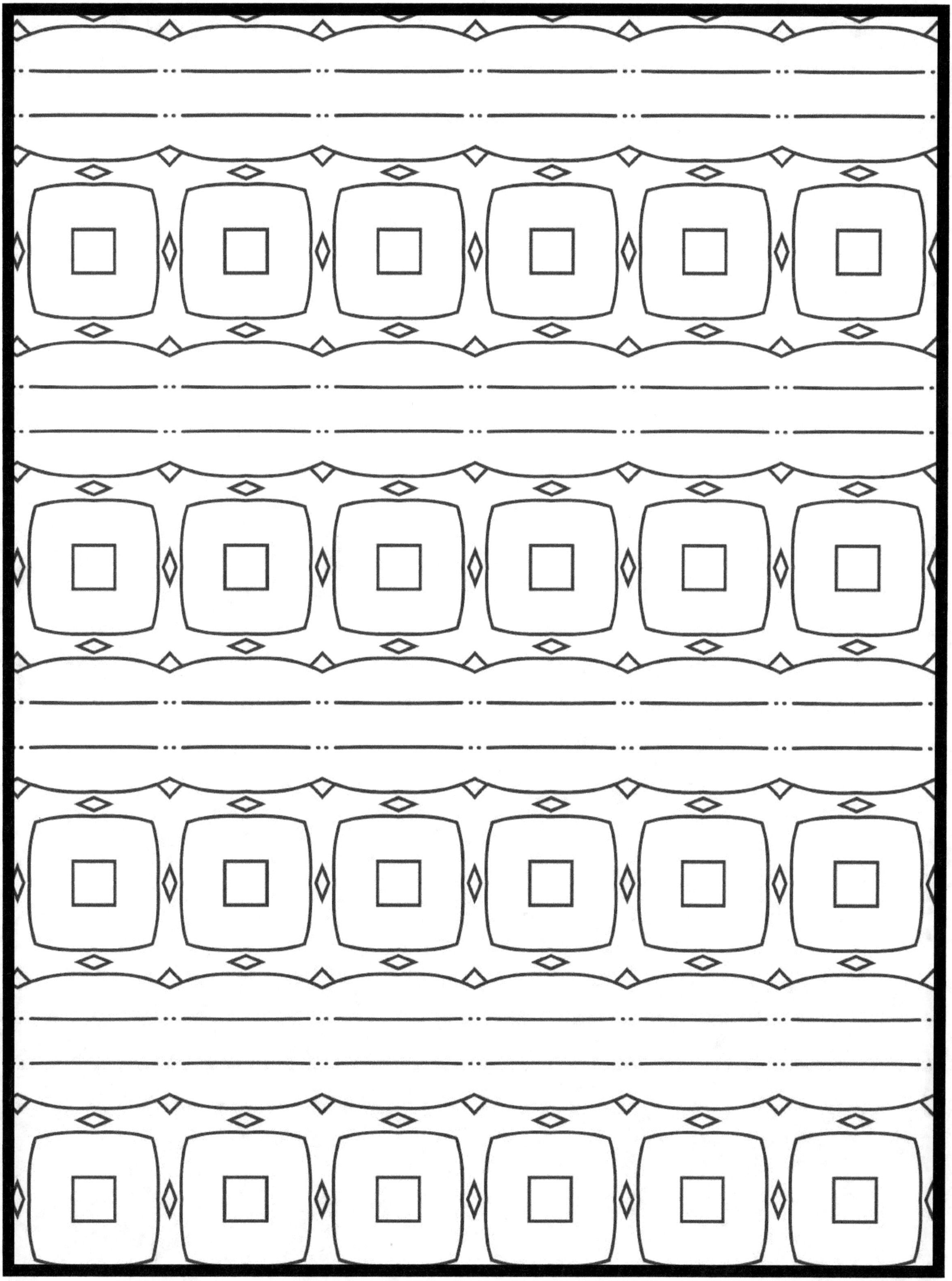

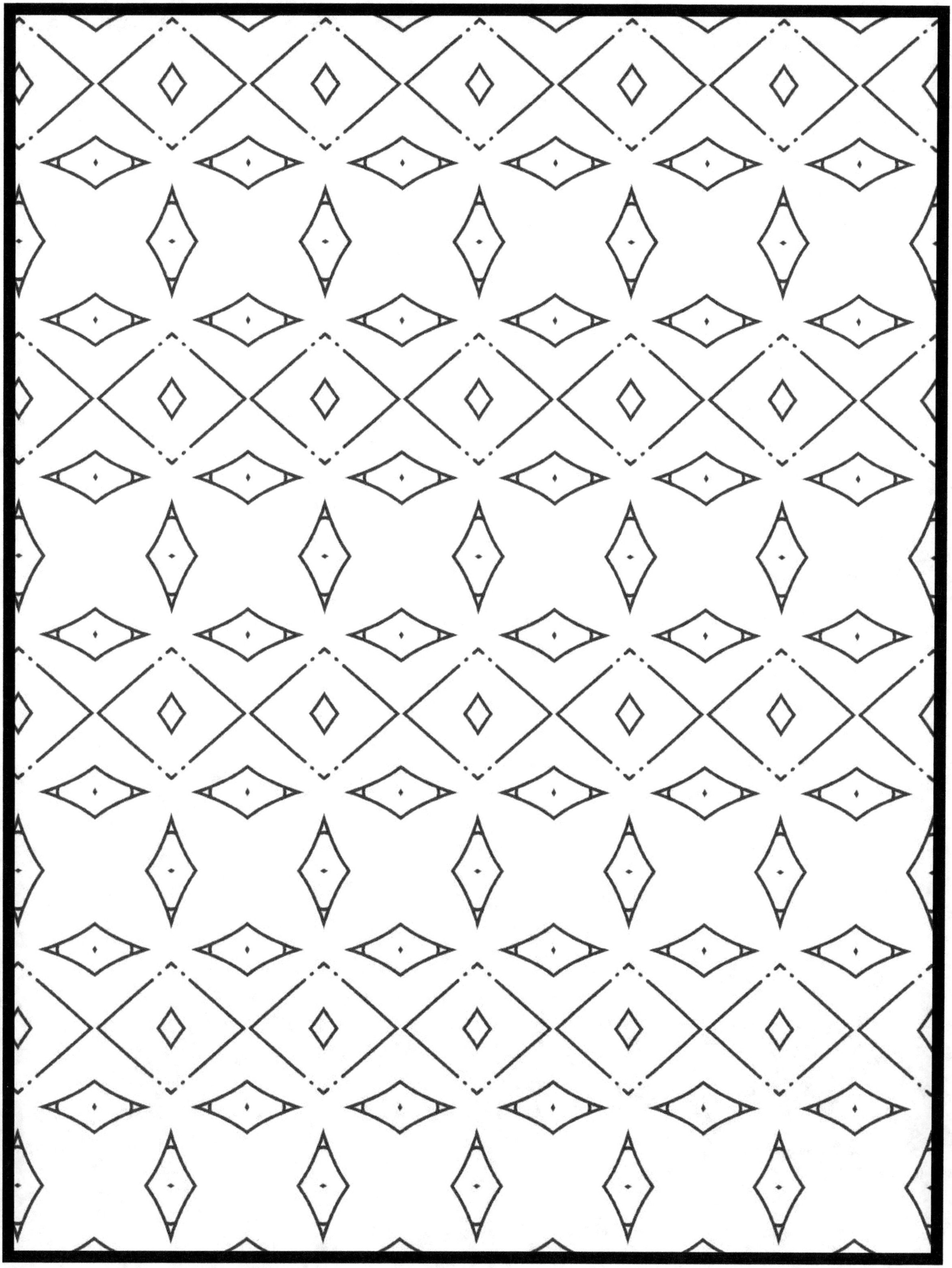

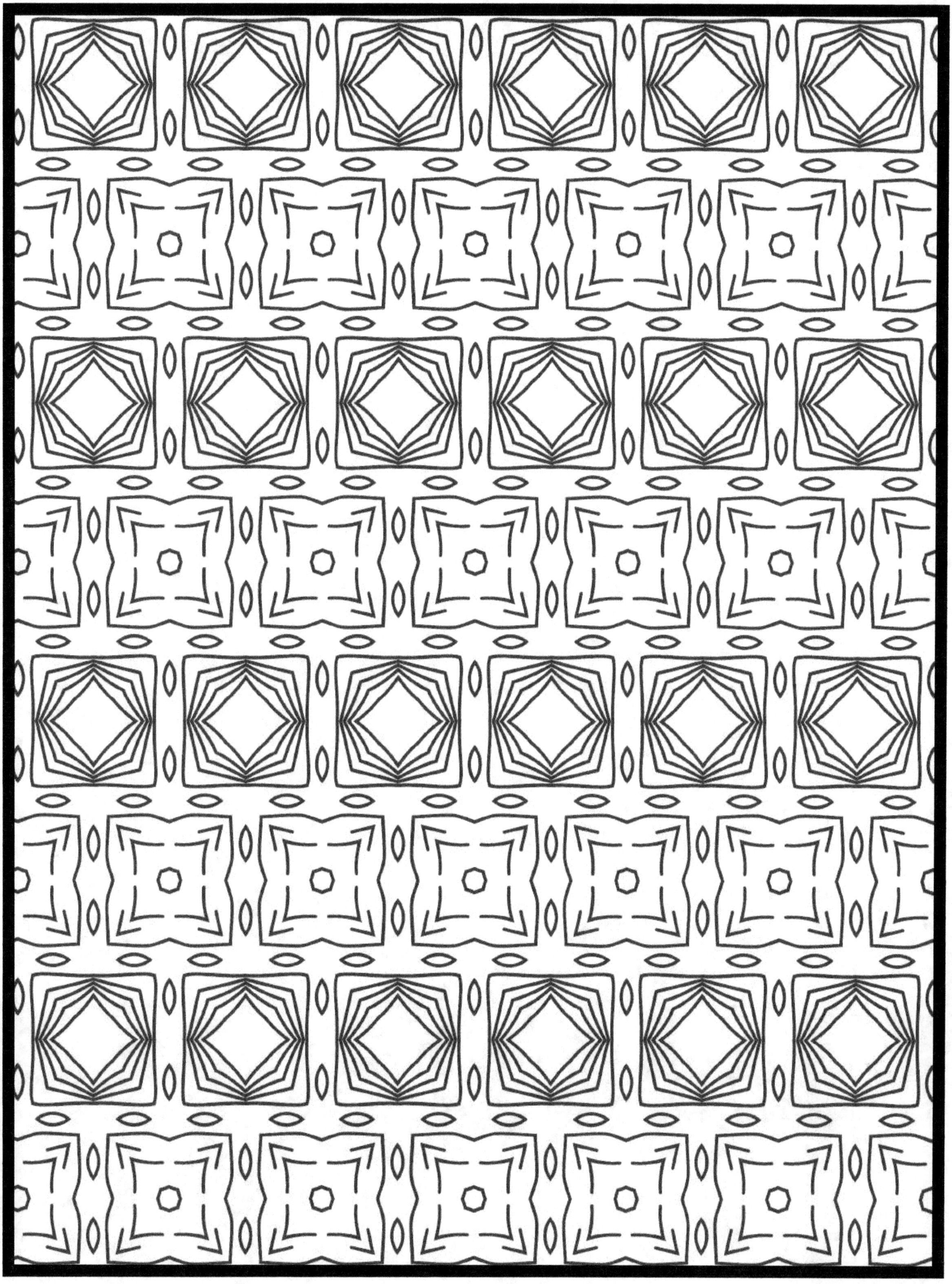

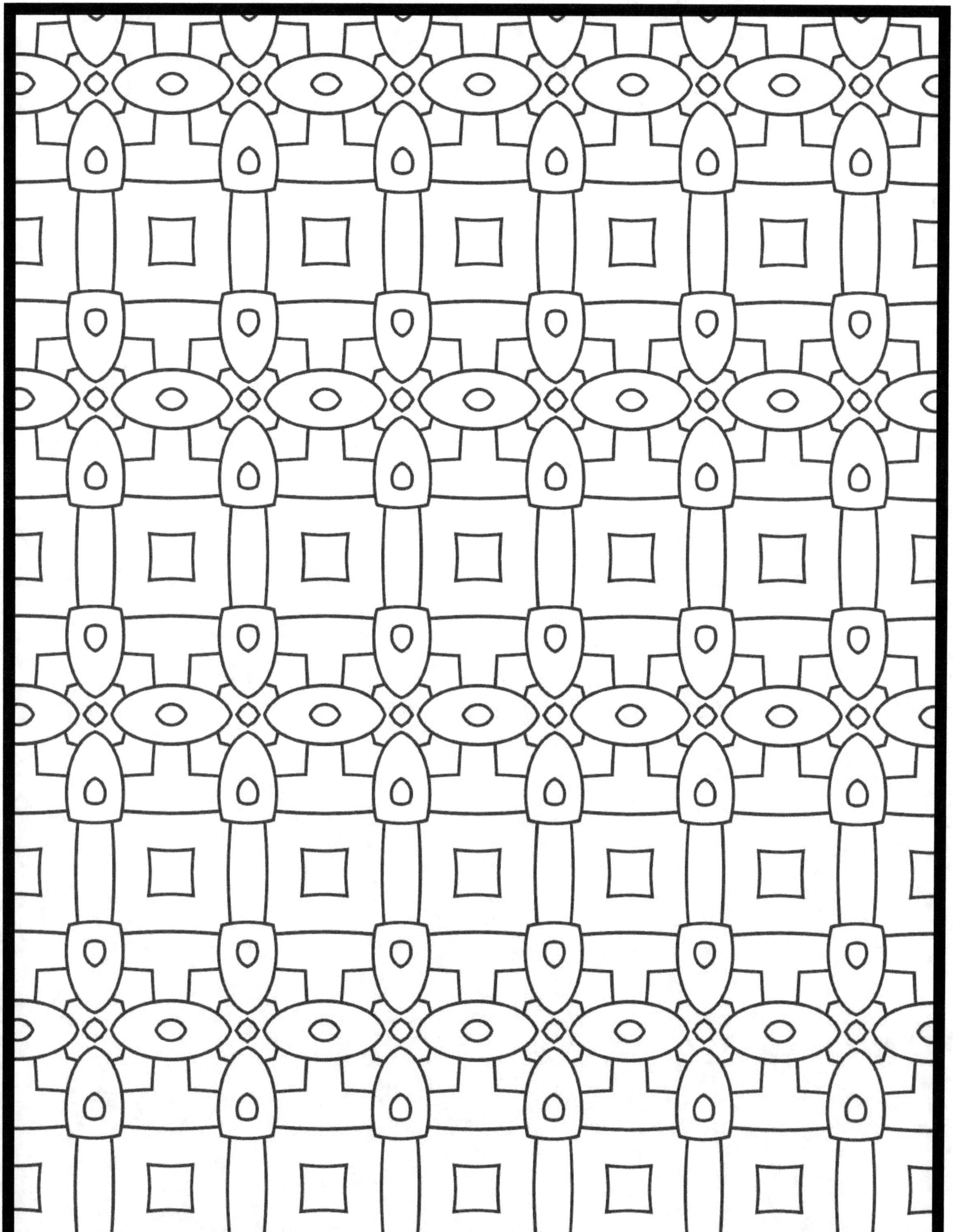

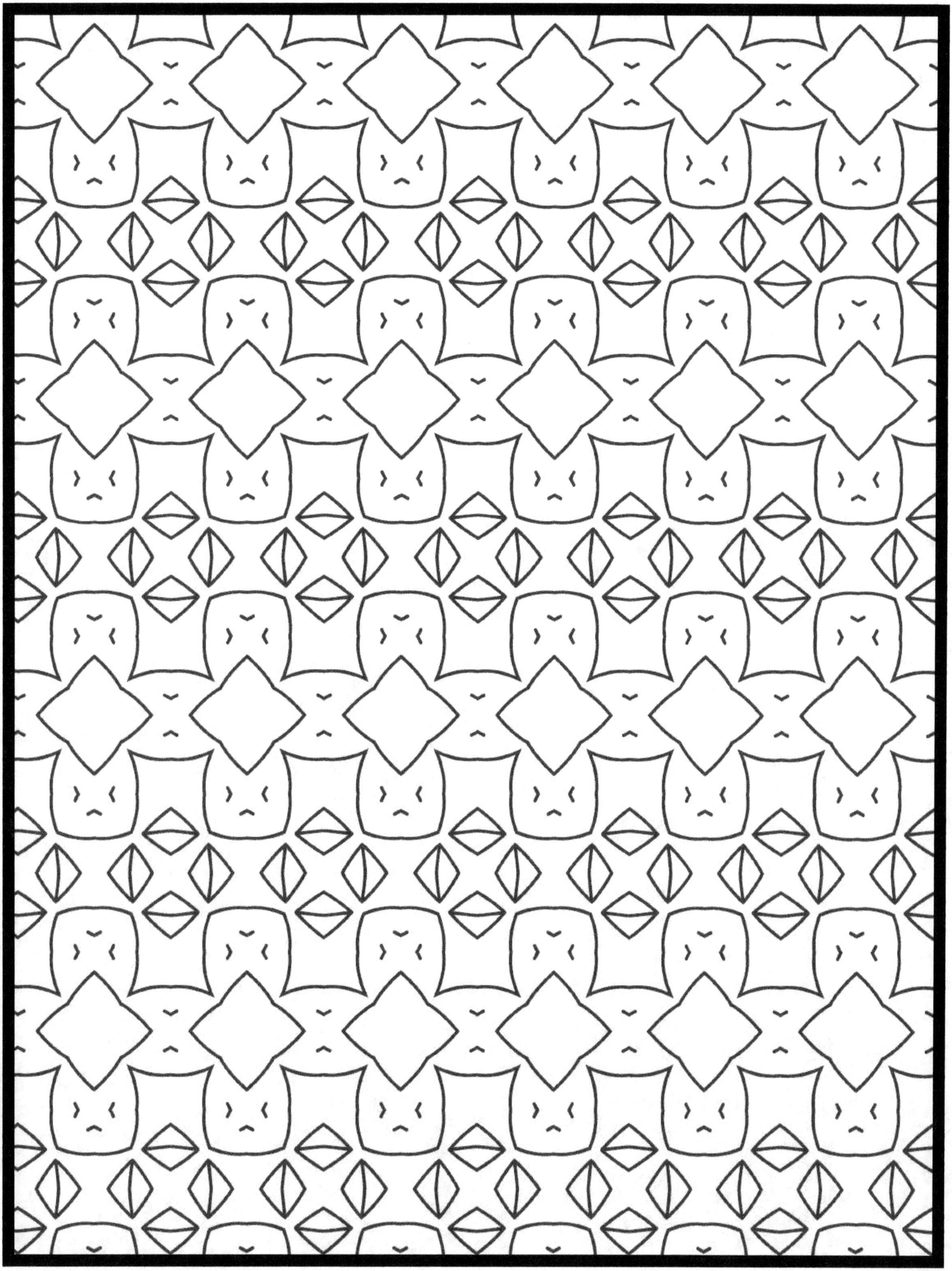

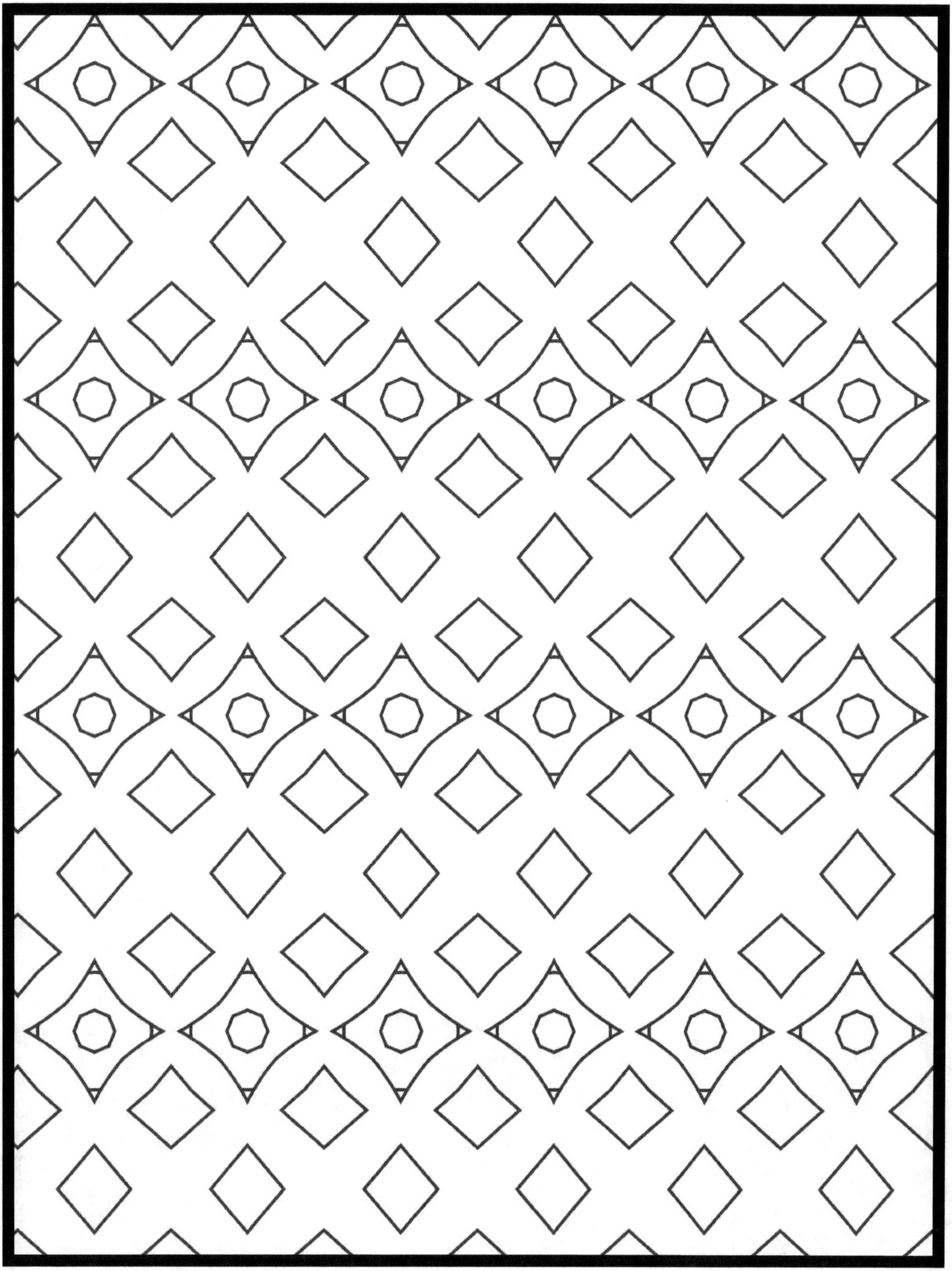

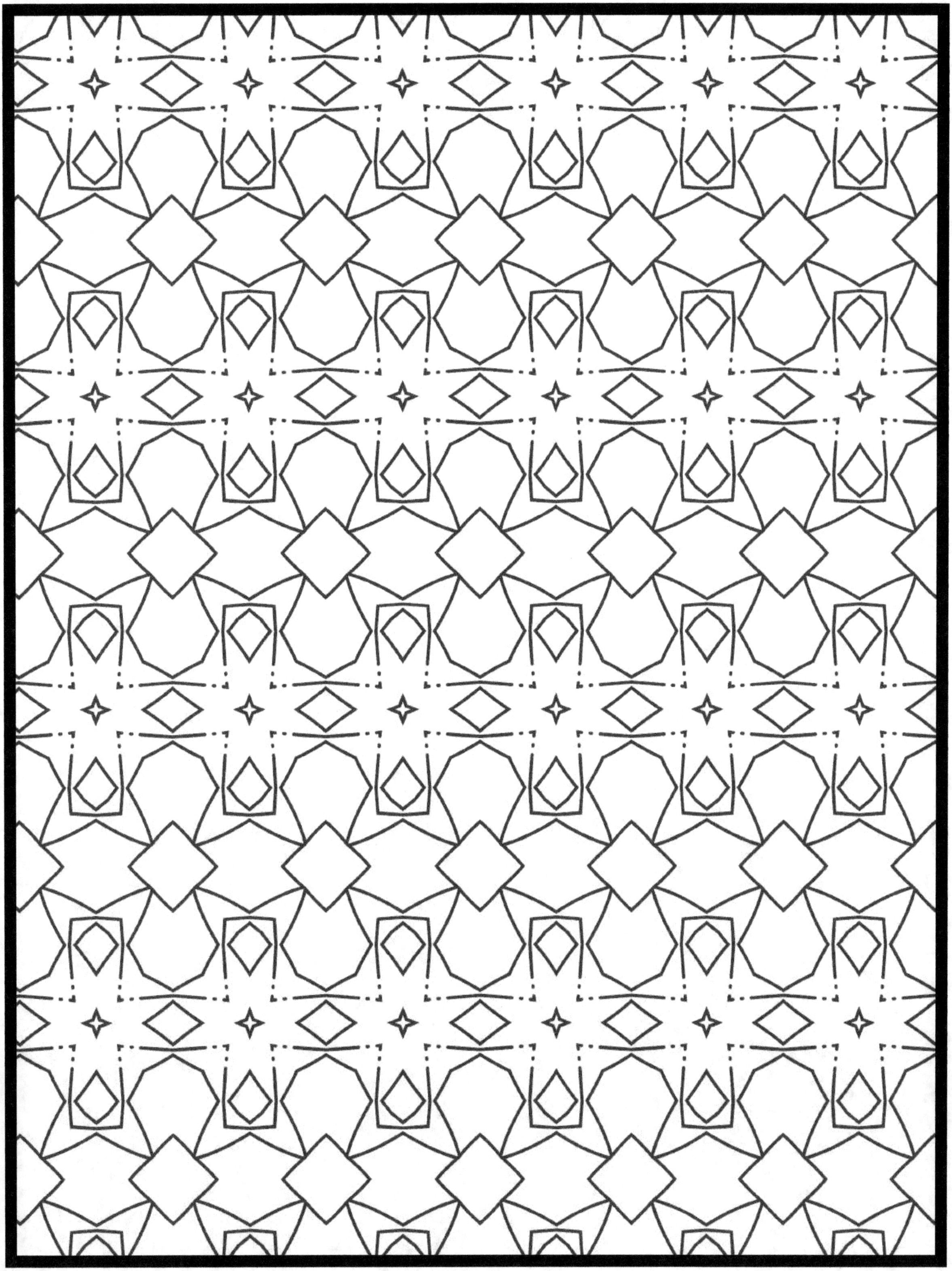

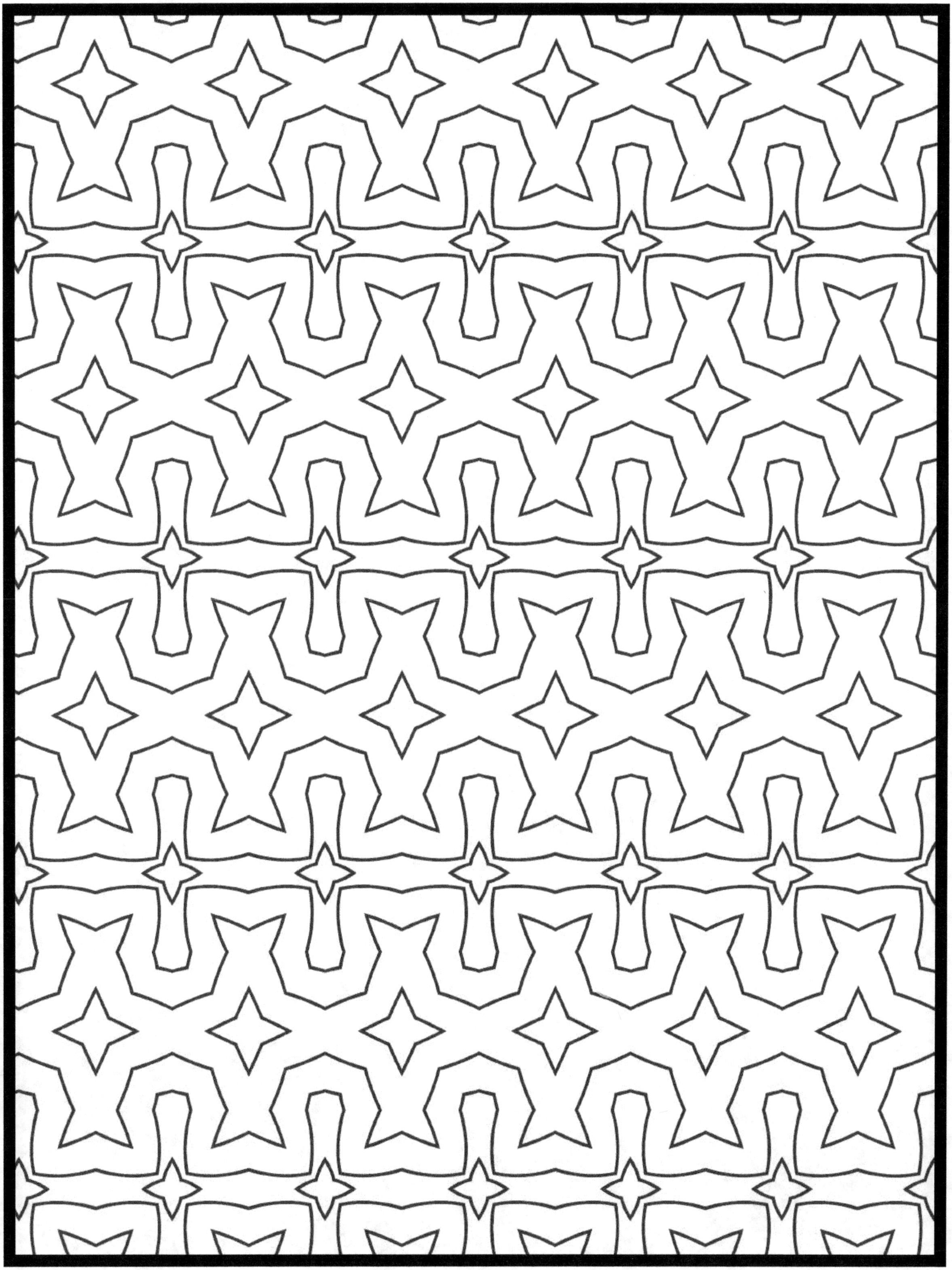

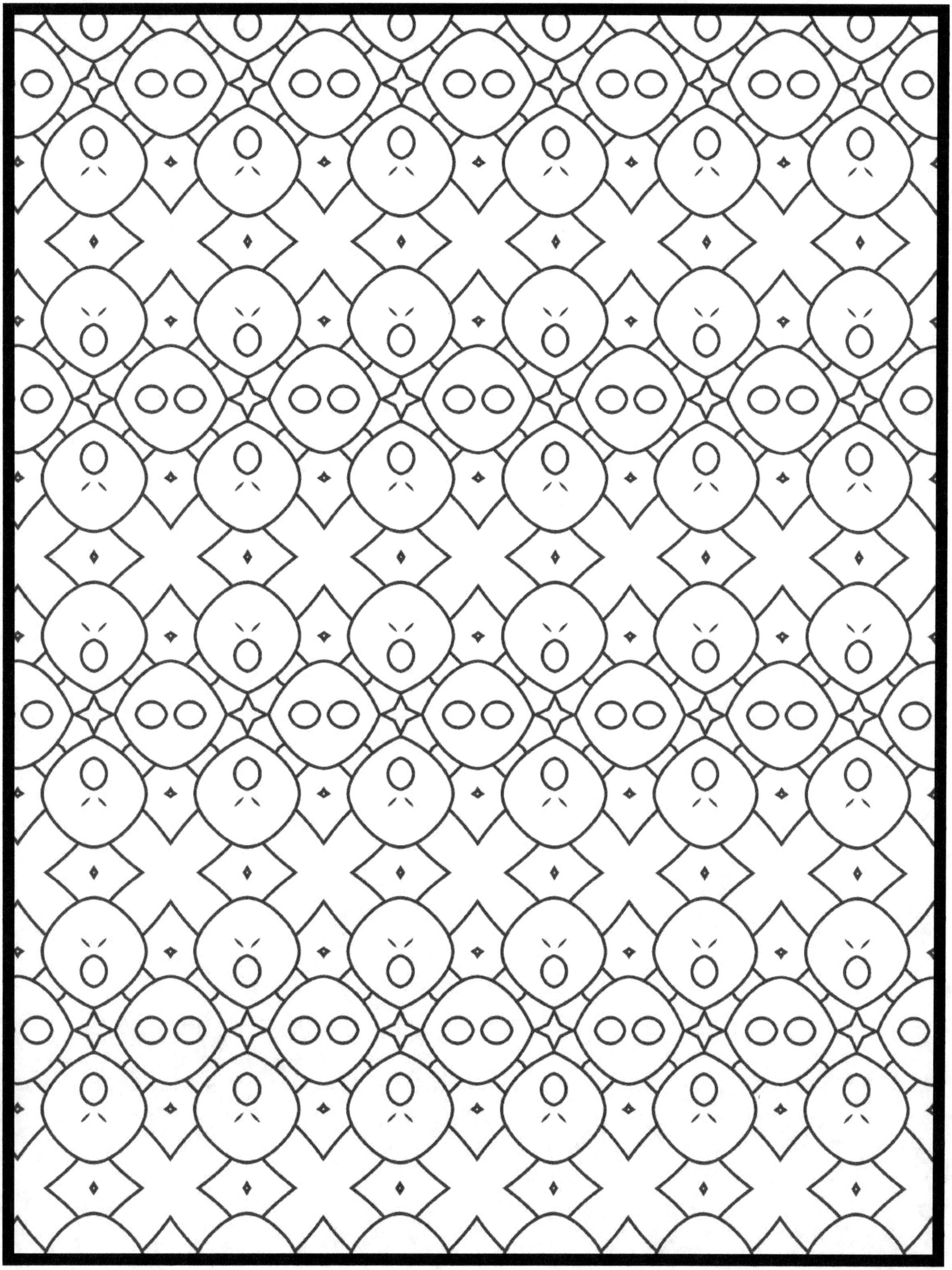

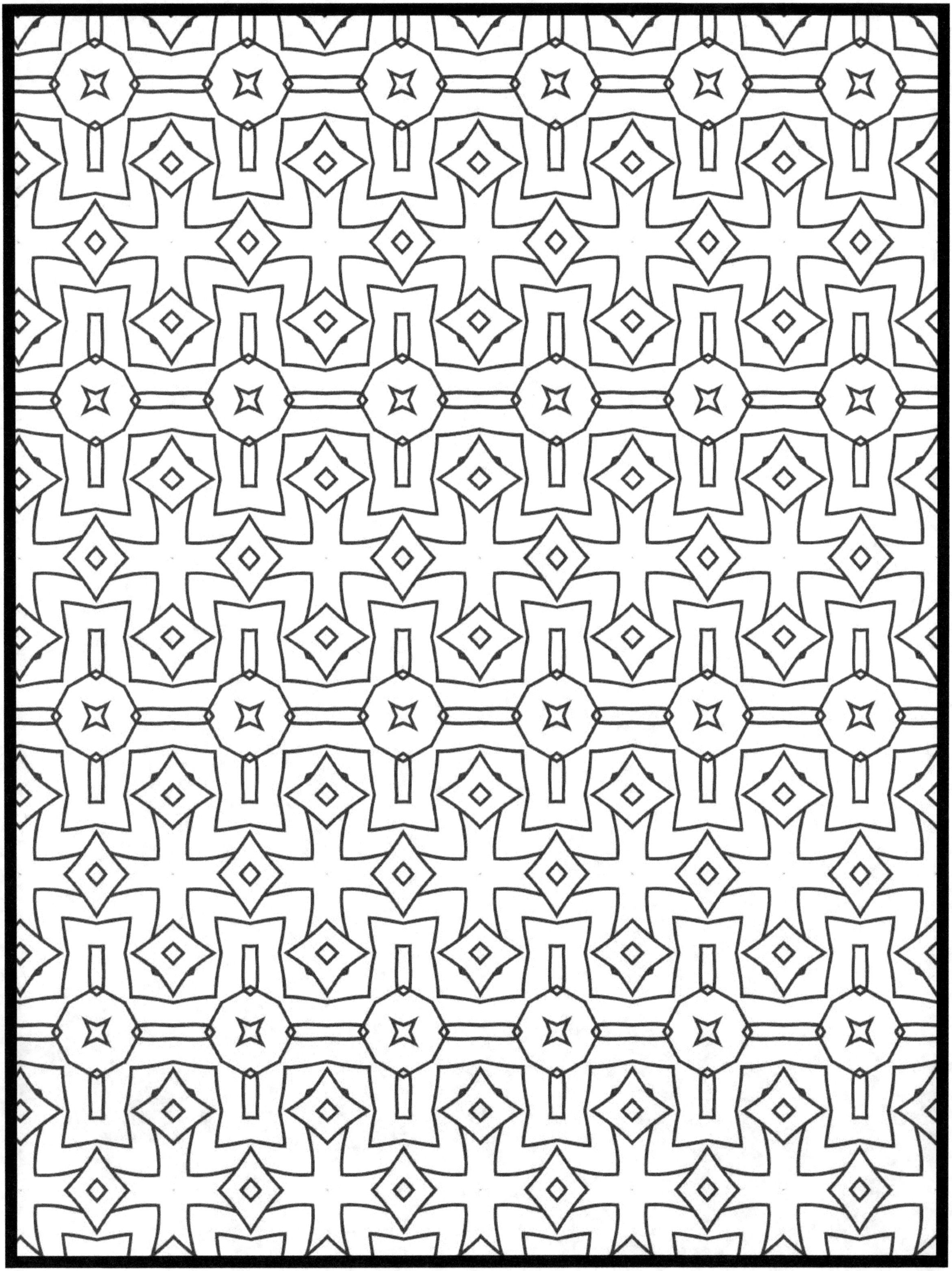

www.ingramcontent.com/pod-product-compliance
Lightning Source LLC
Chambersburg PA
CBHW080844220526
45467CB00008B/2383
* 9 7 9 8 6 9 9 2 5 0 9 1 2 *